PRAISE FOR
LIVING ON PURPOSE

"To say that Amy Wong changed my life would be putting it mildly. Anyone interested in getting out of their way and unlocking their creative reserves should read this book. And then read it again!"

—ANURADHA MURALIDHARAN,
Chief Operating Officer at Expensify

"Who doesn't want to finally feel at home in their own life, relationships, and profession? Amy Wong offers a compelling book to guide you away from self-imposed limitations and toward a path of intention, leading to an authentic and joyous life."

—ADAM GAZZALEY, MD PhD, David Dolby Distinguished
Professor of Neurology, Physiology and Psychiatry & Behavioral Sciences;
Executive Director of Neuroscape at University of California,
San Francisco; coauthor of *The Distracted Mind*

"*Living on Purpose* has taken me by surprise. In a lifetime of exploring the terrain of the human heart and mind, I find Amy Wong's understanding and wisdom to be deeply refreshing. A case in point, Amy illuminates the nature of rejection and its impact throughout our lives in a wholly unique way. Making this discovery in the pages of her book will bring readers closer to themselves and help them to navigate the world with greater openness and freedom. Amy is an emerging teacher whose brilliant light you'll want to keep an eye on."

—BARNET BAIN, author of *The Book of Doing and Being* and
producer of the Oscar-winning film *What Dreams May Come*

"Amy Wong has written a powerful book about what living on purpose truly means. Insightful, candid, and engaging, it's a must-read for anyone ready to go from succeeding by accident to thriving on purpose."

—MIKE ROBBINS, author of *Nothing Changes Until You Do*

"If you've ever desperately wanted something, felt held back by self-doubt, or wondered what was next (i.e. if you're human!), please read this smart, gentle, personal, and *so true* book by Amy Wong on how to live on purpose. Wong's approach is truly original—world-class coach, mathematician, and trusted girlfriend. I love this book. It's a life-changer."

—BETHANY SALTMAN, author of the critically acclaimed *Strange Situation: A Mother's Journey into the Science of Attachment*

"Amy Wong has created a greatly needed and highly practical guide on how to shift foundational perceptions into the inherent confidence, purpose, and joy that lives within all of us—something especially valuable during these challenging times. She gets to the core of what holds people back from living their best lives and presents clear steps to make real change. Read it and experience a profound shift in your personal and professional life."

—OWEN O'KEEFFE, Managing Director and Global Head of Technology M&A at Morgan Stanley

"An incredibly relatable, fun, and practical guide that will lead you away from persistent dissatisfaction and fears of not being or having enough. Read it and share it. It's a game-changer."

—ERICA LOCKHEIMER, Vice President of Engineering at LinkedIn

"Engaging, warm, and empowering, Amy Wong offers a compelling guide to an authentic life of joy and freedom. This book has the power to change our individual and collective lives."

—SHAUNA SHAPIRO, PhD, author of *Good Morning, I Love You: Mindfulness + Self-Compassion Practices to Rewire Your Brain*

"This is a wonderful guidebook. It's a delight to read and filled with relatable insights, easy-to-follow practices, and powerful tools. In a warm and inspiring way, Amy Wong offers an unapologetic road map to getting out of your own way and moving toward a life lived with meaning and intention."

—CHRIS PAN, founder of MyIntent.org

"As a culture, we have numbed ourselves to the ability to lean into our true aspirations and live an authentic life. This eye-opening, moving book will help a lot of people break free from the mental habits that hold them back."

—CHIP CONLEY, founder of Joie de Vivre Hospitality and author of *Wisdom at Work*

"Amy Wong has written a must-read guidebook for anyone wanting to break out of the uncomfortable cycle of 'not enough' and escape from the rat race once and for all."

—DR. DIANA HENDEL, former hospital CEO, executive coach, author of *Responsible: A Memoir*, and coauthor of the award-winning *Trauma to Triumph*

LIVING

On

Purpose

Five **DELIBERATE CHOICES** *to*
Realize **FULFILLMENT** *and* **JOY**

AMY ELIZA WONG

BrainTrust
INK

BrainTrust Ink
Nashville, Tennessee
www.braintrustink.com

This work is being published under the BrainTrust Ink imprint by
an exclusive arrangement with BrainTrust. BrainTrust Ink and the
BrainTrust logos are registered trademarks of BrainTrust. The BrainTrust
Ink logo is a wholly owned trademark of BrainTrust.

Distributed by Greenleaf Book Group

For ordering information or special discounts for bulk purchases, please
contact Greenleaf Book Group at PO Box 91869, Austin, TX 78709,
512.891.6100.

Design and composition by Greenleaf Book Group and Sheila Parr
Cover design by Greenleaf Book Group and Sheila Parr

Publisher's Cataloging-in-Publication data is available.

Print ISBN: 978-1-956072-02-0

eBook ISBN: 978-1-956072-03-7

Part of the Tree Neutral® program, which offsets the number of trees
consumed in the production and printing of this book by taking proactive
steps, such as planting trees in direct proportion to the number of trees
used: www.treeneutral.com

Printed in the United States of America on acid-free paper

22 23 24 25 26 27   10 9 8 7 6 5 4 3 2 1

First Edition

For my mom and dad,
who fanned the flames of my passions,
guided me when the path wasn't clear,
and trusted me to follow my instincts
when it was.

CONTENTS

FOREWORD

*C*an you imagine a world where each of us awoke each day with a feeling of deep engagement in our lives? A world where self-compassion, honesty, and connection were the norm? Can you imagine yourself waking up every day with an inner feeling of true joy and happy anticipation—the kind of feeling you had as a child on a special day of celebration?

Do you remember having days when you couldn't wait to get out of bed to see what magic was about to happen?

That kind of excitement comes from knowing and honoring what's true for you at your very core. And while many of us start out with an unbroken connection to ourselves, very often this way of living gets fractured, and we begin to live a life that isn't authentically our own. We do this for various reasons. We have rent or a mortgage to pay. We must feed and clothe ourselves. We may have other mouths to feed, including our beloved dogs and cats. For most of us, as we set off on our own as young adults, our primary reason for getting a "j.o.b." is to take care of our basic survival needs. We live the lives we do, and then sometime down the road, many of us find ourselves standing on a precipice—surveying where we have come to—asking ourselves, "How the heck did I get here?" Maybe all we've been doing is living the life that's in front of us, the one that meets our needs, rather than the one that feeds our souls. Something is missing, and there's a nagging question: What is that "something"? A sense of meaning? Optimism? Purpose? Passion?

As you embarked on your personal journey, driven in part by fulfilling your basic needs, passion and purpose may not have been high on your priority list. But things are different now. Now, you may find yourself on a path that's leading you to destinations new and unknown. And while you may not have even noticed yourself taking the turns in the road, here you are—called toward something deeper. This is exactly the moment when a guide comes in handy—someone who knows the terrain and can help you navigate it with sure footing because they have just the map and compass you need. That's where Amy Wong comes in. Amy has a well-developed map and a compass made of great courage, wisdom, compassion, and humor. She has walked the walk before you and can help you along the path ahead as you traverse unknown territory.

I met Amy on a birthday sail around the San Francisco Bay for a mutual friend of ours. She's the kind of woman I instantly connect with. She is confident, kind, and vibrantly alive. Definitely the life of the party! She has that "it" factor that makes someone a shining star—*a rock star*. As I spoke with Amy that day, we talked about her desire to write a book. While she humbly described her work with high profile corporations and tech giants (as a coach, speaker, and trainer), I was truly wowed by her experience and accomplishments. But honestly, it was her authenticity that struck me the most. It was clear to me why companies hire her to speak about and teach the intricacies of communication and leadership skills. Today, as a good friend, I continue to marvel at the power and depth of Amy's communication in matters of business and life in general. Her love of family and the work she does oozes from her with the kind happiness that is contagious.

As you read this book, you will find that you have at your side a wonderful coach in the process of shifting your inner world. Amy deeply understands the psychological, emotional, and spiritual journey that you're on and how to overcome the obstacles and fears that most of us face along the way. In *Living on Purpose*, Amy shows the way to a truth that you know in your heart of hearts—that the one clear path to joy is in being yourself. She reawakens the knowing that who you are right here and now is enough. You don't have to go looking to find anything on the outside because where the magic happens is in realizing who you are on the inside.

If it feels like it's time to take a serious and solid look at how to find and walk a new path—one that gives you freedom no matter what you are doing—then Amy has given you the road map here. You can move along from the edge where you may be merely surviving and make the choices that will allow you to thrive. *Living on Purpose* is a guidebook for living a life of real joy and creating more magic in your life. And I can tell you that it's never too late. It's never too late to turn inward to find that sense of inner meaning and delight. Turning inward is the key because it is what's inside that will alter your very reality on the outside and change your feelings about everything.

You need not wait another day for this quality of life, but sometimes you may find yourself waiting, nonetheless. My late husband Dr. Richard Carlson, author of *Don't Sweat the Small Stuff,* called it the "if only . . . then" syndrome. We live under the illusion that if we achieve our worldly goals, then we will find happiness. This illusive pattern befalls the smartest, most psychologically sophisticated people, keeping even those who appear to have everything stuck with feelings of dissatisfaction and longing. "If only . . . then" keeps us chasing after what is always just outside our reach. Meanwhile, as we're looking for and waiting for the next thing (and the next and the next), we're left with an emptiness because, If I may paraphrase John Lennon, life is what foes on around you while you're occupied making other plans."

What kind of life do you want to be living right now? When you come to the last moments of your life, are you going to settle for saying, "If only I had another day?" Is the manner in which you are living serving you well? And most of all, are you living a life to be treasured? In the pages ahead, Amy will help you to answer questions like these as you learn the power of deliberate choice. So, prepare yourself, because you're about to start making choices that free you to live a life that's overflowing with meaning, purpose, and lasting joy.

Treasure the gifts of life and love,

—KRISTINE CARLSON,
coauthor of the *New York Times* bestselling
Don't Sweat the Small Stuff series

AN INTRODUCTION

As human beings, our job in life is to help people realize how rare
and valuable each one of us really is, that each of us has something
that no one else has—or will have; something inside that is unique
to all time. It's our job to encourage each other to discover that
uniqueness and to provide ways of developing its expression.

—FRED ROGERS

"*A*my, I got it. I know what you should title your book." This
is what Kim, my friend and coaching colleague, said to me
as she finished writing both our names in huge Arial-like
font on the large whiteboard. That morning we were preparing a conference room for a day-long public speaking training that we would
together facilitate for the company Stripe, in downtown San Francisco. After she turned to look at me, she paused. Using exactly the
body language expected from a skillful communication coach, she
spread her hands apart in the air as if to reveal the most brilliant of
all ideas and thoughtfully offered: "Irrefutable: A Former Mathematician's Objective Guide to Subjective Personal Development."

Before I wrote *this* book, I wanted to write *a* book, and I talked a
lot about it to my friends and family. I think, maybe, that was my way
of putting myself on the hook to bring it into existence. But it wasn't

just any book I wanted to write. I had a lot of ideas on what to focus on and exactly how I would approach it, but the endgame was always the same: it would be a book that mapped out the process to free oneself to live their best life . . . irrefutably.

Yet despite all my casual book brainstorming with anyone who would entertain me, I knew in my heart exactly what I would do—I would combine my personal journey of transformation, thousands of conversations I've had with my coaching clients for more than ten years within my coaching practice, Always On Purpose, and insights and research from specific academic fields. From all of this I would create an indisputable map showing a clear way out of self-sabotage and suffering and into a life *lived on purpose*—into the best version of ourselves.

But let's face it, there are lots of books out there that try to accomplish this. What, in my mind, made my book different from all the other self-help books out there?

Well, I'd pull upon my training as a mathematician to use the principles of logic and sound argument to lead my readers away from limitation and doubt and into authenticity, joy, freedom, and possibilities. Treating personal growth like a math proof, I would present observations, hypotheses, and truths in such a way that my readers would derive for themselves the logical conclusion that they were already whole and complete.

Now, clearly, I didn't end up with Kim's endearing and witty title suggestion. If I had, you might not have picked up this book and read this far! Which is to say that while this book isn't a treatise on personal transformation (and doesn't at all read like a math book, promise!), it does provide a clear map out of "surviving" and into "thriving" by learning to access and harness your superpower of *choice*.

What's the deal with "choice," you may wonder? Why and how is choice a source of such great power?

The most concise answer I can give you is this: because everyone wants to feel good. Yet everyone struggles with an inner dialogue that, a lot of times, doesn't feel good. We all want to thrive. Yet we sustain a set of habits based on our inner dialogue that keeps us from doing just that.

But here is a truth that can set us free: we're *choosing* our inner dialogue and we're *choosing* our habits.

While we could choose thoughts and actions that give us the good feelings we want, quite often we choose the ones that keep us stuck, stressed out, and repeating painful patterns.

What gives? Why do we make choices daily that are in direct opposition to what we really want?

This burning question is one that has fueled the work I do—the work I love. Over the past ten years, I've had the privilege of coaching the most diverse and amazing souls imaginable on the topics of life, leadership, and communication. I've had the honor and the pleasure of going on the deepest and most profound journeys of transformation with people whose backgrounds range from college students, fellow coaches, therapists, celebrities, single working parents, professional athletes, entrepreneurs, recovering addicts, law enforcement, lawyers, doctors, teachers, scientists, investment bankers, executives in companies of some of the largest household names, and founders and CEOs of successful start-ups.

I've had the honor to coach people who want to make the most of their lives. People with desires. People with fears. People with histories, memories, tragedies, traumas, secrets, questions, hopes, longings, and dreams.

People just like you.

Thousands of clients have taken my hand and led me deep into their inner worlds. So I'm not kidding when I say I've been blessed with a behind-the-scenes look into our humanity. With all I've heard and seen, I've decided that none of us are immune to self-imposed suffering. Despite the pretty facades or perfectly curated Instagram feeds, each of us struggle in our own way. And often we do so in silence, assuming we're the only one that deals with a heavy dose of self-doubt, shame, jealousy, fear, anxiety, or—fill in the blank accordingly. Despite the apparent wealth, perfect relationship, or enviable job title, there is both a desire and a struggle to feel *true peace*—to feel at home in our minds, hearts, and bodies; to feel like our life is exactly the way it was meant to be.

And we're mainly struggling with ourselves, believing that the changes we wish to make are just out of reach.

"If only I could . . ."

"If only I had the ability to . . ."

"If only I knew how to . . ."

"If only I could figure out what . . ."

"If only I could finally achieve that final thing that tells me *I've arrived.*"

If there was one thing I could shout from the rooftops, it would be, "You are not alone!"

These distressing thoughts are most definitely experienced by your neighbor, your colleague, your boss, your mail person, your mom, your sibling, and that stranger in the grocery store who beat you to the shortest checkout line. The exact contents of your fear and struggle are obviously different than theirs, but the intensity, meaning, and impact are all similarly felt.

Yes, you are not alone. And for every one of us there is a way to become free of this kind of internal tyranny. I am certain of this because I see it happen on a regular basis. People are reclaiming their power and joy. And you can too.

A ROADMAP THAT CAN CHANGE THE COURSE OF YOUR LIFE

I am not a licensed therapist. I am not a scientist. I am a transformational coach who cares deeply about people and the quality of life they create for themselves. For as long as I can remember, I've been devoted to exploring these questions: Why are we here? How do we make sense of all this? What does it mean to thrive? I provide frameworks and specific mindsets that help one out of self-imposed limitation and into the practice of *living on purpose*—into a life of joy, inner calm, and freedom.

Although I am not a professional researcher, I lean on research initiated from my fascinations, drawing correlations from my own experience and the reported experiences of countless others. I make distinctions where distinctions aren't readily found. And while I don't pretend for a second that what I say is the end-all, be-all, I do have a roadmap to offer—a roadmap composed of five extraordinary choices that, separately and together, will guide you to the life you were uniquely born to live.

The best reasons I know of to take this map and make it your own are because:

You want to feel good.
You want to feel free.
You want to feel whole.
You want to feel at peace.

Though these statements may not be objective truths, I treat them as such. I believe that every person on the planet desires to feel settled, at peace, significant, loved, loving, and purposeful. That all of us want to feel free, empowered, and capable of doing and achieving whatever we put our minds to. But sometimes that's easier said than done, right? As basic as this all sounds, we end up getting in our own way somehow.

I should know. As you'll learn in Part I of this book, I've struggled with own my fair share of self-imposed suffering. And given my backstage pass into the inner workings of many other lives, I've observed multiple forms of self-imposed limitation from every angle. With this exposure, I've narrowed down the nature of our challenge.

Our challenge is an internal oppositional force—a kind of internal dialogue and feeling—that perpetuates a false narrative about who we are, what we deserve, and what we're capable of. What gets in the way of the life we were born to live—that life of joy, possibilities, and freedom—is the little part of us in the corner of our mind that tenaciously argues for our limitations and ruminates on everything that could go wrong.

Regardless of how far along you are in your life or how much you've already accomplished, chances are you contend with this oppositional force on occasion. You might describe this inner struggle as a subtle feeling of not being enough—not good enough, not competent enough, or not accomplished enough, *yet*. Maybe someday, but not yet. Maybe you're tired of not being able to put a finger on why you're not as fulfilled as you could or should be. Your life might look pretty good on paper, but you continue to look to the external world to fill a void.

Maybe you strive for more money, a promotion, a bigger house, a new partner, or maybe a Bordeaux-colored Maserati. Perhaps it's another Hermes Limited Edition handbag. Whatever you secure is fulfilling for a short time, sure, but it's ultimately hollow and unfulfilling. And in a resigned and somewhat defeated way, you reach for more. For something different. For something better. Simply because you're used to doing just that.

But you can't get away from that nagging feeling. The one that's hinting to you it's not more stuff you need—like a seat at the table, a promotion, or another degree. It's hinting at the possibility that you may have internal roadblocks to true inner peace and freedom. You just don't know what to do differently to dismantle those roadblocks. And worse, tackling the required change to the psyche might feel like such a big, complicated problem and time-consuming process that it's easier to distract yourself with newer shiny things, titles, or accolades. Instinctively, you might sense that this could be so significant that if you really did something about it, everything that truly matters to you could change in a moment—values, priorities, goals, and even relationships. That potentially earth-shaking paradigm shift feels scary.

We generally don't like to be scared. Most of us don't like uncertainty. Many of us would rather stick with what we know, in discomfort, than risk entering the unknown for the possibility of freedom on the other side.

Insanity is doing the same thing over and over again and expecting different results.

—USUALLY ATTRIBUTED TO ALBERT EINSTEIN

This challenge—this internal oppositional force—signals that we're tolerating limiting or unhelpful beliefs about who we are and what life is about. It's exactly what gets in the way of the life we were each born to live. It's a problem.

If any one of these rings true for you, then you're familiar with the problem:

- You can't figure out what you could do differently—more of or less of—to feel more accomplished, fulfilled, and at peace.

- You feel behind, stressed about everything you should have done or what you should be doing right now.

- You're overscheduled and have a hard time saying no.

- You regret some of your past decisions and judge yourself on your mistakes and failures.

- You compare yourself to others.

- You're sometimes afraid to speak up, to take a stand, to "take up space."

- You hold yourself back from anything you could potentially fail at.

- You can take things personally.

- You realize you're judgmental of others at times, and though you know it doesn't serve you, you do it anyway.

- You feel isolated from others at times.

- You have a hard time opening up to and trusting others.

- There are certain situations where you lose your ability to communicate clearly.

- You experience a lack of ambition or clarity about what you want to do in the world.

- "Who am I to _____ ?" is a statement you use to hold yourself back.

- You're worried about what people think of you.

- Consumed with image and appearance, you feel you need to look or show up a certain way to be accepted.

- You have "survival mechanisms" to play it safe.

- Forgiveness can be hard for you.

- You look to someone else or need someone else to make you feel complete and worthy.

- You feel as though you're in a rat race, always trying to achieve, win, or look the part. Your life is all about achieving the next big thing to feel better.

- You wish you were more brave or courageous than you feel you are now.

- You're afraid to be vulnerable.

- Your inner critic keeps you from choices that would delight you.

- You're afraid of being found out, secretly worried that others will learn the truth about you.

- You're tired of sensing that you're holding yourself back, and you just can't put your finger on why.

Divided into three sections, this book provides a map out of all this and back to your true *self*. It's a map for going on the adventure to discover your authentic power and reuniting with the whole and complete person you lost contact with (to one degree or another) in navigating the complexities of relationships and life. Using examples from my own journey of transformation and examples of my clients' breakdowns and breakthroughs, this book teaches you how to exercise five distinct choices to feel good, free, whole, and at peace on a regular basis.

- **Part I: The Power of Deliberate Choices** provides a foundation for understanding the power of choice. Here I share my own dark nights and luminous awakenings, as well as the true tales of quiet triumph of some of my clients (all names changed unless otherwise noted). In this section I offer the first three choices, which marks your transition from a life stumbled into by accident to one that is lived on purpose.

- **Part II: Discover the Life You Were Born to Live** takes the conversation deeper, defining the root of self-imposed suffering as *inner opposition*, an internal force that keeps us from inner peace, joy, and fulfillment. While proposing the underlying mechanism that causes it, I offer a process to derive for yourself how you personally hold yourself back through your own inner opposition. Not only will Part II help you to clearly see who you are *not*, with the unveiling of Choice #4 you will be one step closer to who you really are.

- **Part III: Making the Ultimate Choice** is the turning point. After learning four of the five deliberate choices in the previous sections, you are now primed with a greater understanding of your own complexity and are ready to address the final challenge: *how to exercise the ultimate choice.* Here, too, I guide you through the predicament that knowledge of choice is not enough and usher you through the perceptual shift necessary to embody Choice #5—the final choice that has the power to free you from the rat race and ground you in the truth of you.

Concluding each chapter is a running checklist of the five choices, as well as the correlated processes, practices, and exercises we've covered up until that point. By the end of the journey, you'll have a roadmap to call your own, one that leads you to your unique life lived *on purpose.*

THE GREATEST JOY AWAITS YOU

Now, "purpose" is a rather loaded word. Our minds usually go straight to "purpose" as a *noun*—a simple "thing" that captures a complex and often intimidating idea:

"What's my purpose?"
"How do I find my purpose?" and
"Oh my God, what if I don't have a purpose?"

As a life and executive coach, I field these questions regularly. And while purpose in this context enthralls me, that singular sense of purpose—like discovering that your calling is to build regenerative technologies addressing climate change—is not what this book is about. (Although it's possible that the result of going through this book may lead to the clarity that allows for that kind of realization!) This book is largely born out of the philosophy of my coaching practice, Always On Purpose, and is about living and being *on purpose*—recalibrating to purpose as an adverb rather than a noun, where the focus is less about *what* you achieve and more about *how* you experience your precious and beautiful life. It's more about the quality of your experience than the tangible goods (although the tangibles become all the more sweet as you begin to feel a greater affection for your daily life experience). It's about thriving *on purpose* through intentional choices, as opposed to stumbling into feeling good on occasion, by accident. In this way, it's about engaging with your life *deliberately*, which boils down to being fully and boldly aligned behind the important choices you make, with no resistance or contradicting energy.

There really is no greater joy than creating on purpose, living on purpose—being *always* on purpose. Which simply means that you are at the helm of your own ship, well-equipped to handle the conditions of the sea, fearlessly transforming unchartered territory into an adventure of your own design. To live *on purpose* means to actively create, own, and celebrate your current and emerging reality through the agency of choice. When you deliberately choose your thoughts, words, and actions, you are in the driver's seat of your own life.

But to be *always* on purpose requires intentional choice one level deeper, at the level of perception. When you consciously choose your interpretation about what life is about, how it works, and who you *really* are, you can unleash the joyful and free soul within, the one you were born to live. And that is what this book is here to do: guide you through the practice of living on purpose back to your true self.

YOUR COMMITMENT IS THE GAME-CHANGER

All told, this book exists because I wholeheartedly agree with Fred Rogers—our job is to help others realize the truth of their being: *how rare and valuable each one of us really is.* The five choices that make up a living-on-purpose life are here for you exactly for this reason. And making these choices deliberately, it turns out, is not a one-shot deal. It's a rich life practice that deepens through experience and time. If you can commit to keeping an open heart and an open mind throughout these pages, I promise that this journey back to your self will unfold delightfully, revealing powerful truth in the adage: the most important relationship you will ever have is the one you have with yourself.

LIVING ON

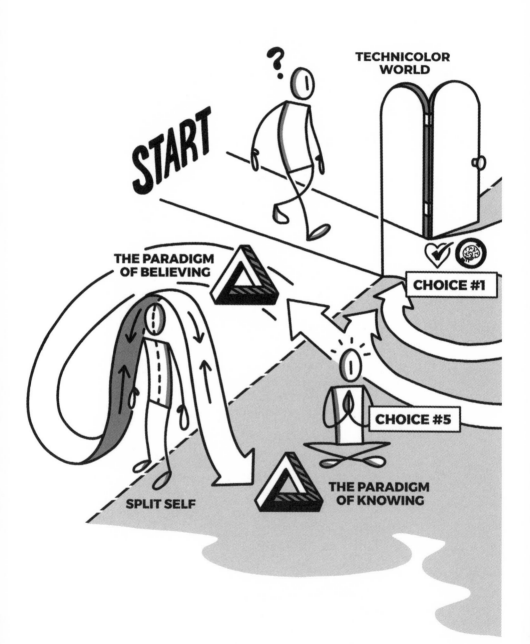

PURPOSE MAP

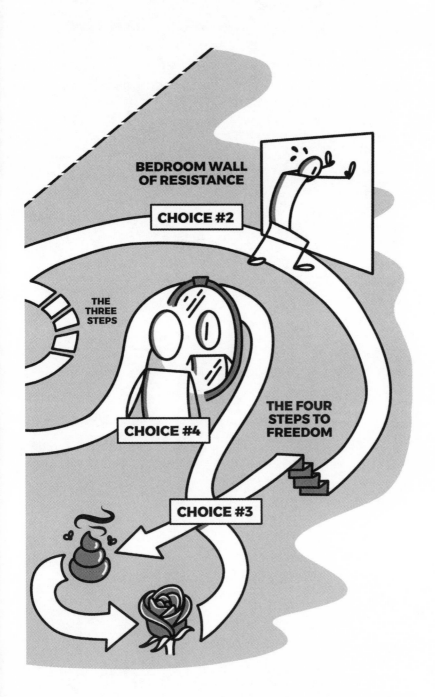

Part I

THE POWER OF
DELIBERATE CHOICES

Chapter 1

OPENING THE DOOR TO A
TECHNICOLOR WORLD

I give up. *You* show me the way.

I don't consider myself to be special, gifted, clairvoyant, or anything like that. I actually wish I was. Instead, I'm pretty average. I'm 5'4" and fall right at the average for anything that could be measured by stats, both intellectually and physically. As comforting as that may sound, I never appreciated that as a kid. I always secretly craved the novelty of an aberration. When my eye exam would come back normal, I'd be bummed I didn't get to pick out a pair of glasses with my mom that afternoon. When I started getting chronic headaches in high school, I hoped for some exotic diagnosis so I would have something exciting to tell my friends. Boringly, it turned out to be a sensitivity to aspartame. Convinced that I was going to knock the SATs out of the park, I didn't. At all. I came in exactly at the national average.

There was this *one* time though. I had an allergic reaction to the pain medication I was given when I had my wisdom teeth pulled out. Being swept out of my bed by three handsome paramedics would have been the most epic experience of my sixteen-year-old life . . . if I wasn't consumed with the horrifying worry that I wasn't wearing pajama pants. (Fortunately, I was.)

Allergic reaction aside, I've had a good life from the very beginning, filled with love from family and friends and relatively drama-free. But during a summer day in August of 2008, something happened to me that catapulted me into a completely different paradigm than I had been living previously. I liken it to the original *Wizard of Oz*, when sepia-toned Dorothy Gale opens the door of her farmhouse into the Technicolor world of Oz. My shift felt that dramatic.

Before I take you into this Technicolor world of mine, I need to give you a bit of context. I'm a wife and a mom. Raising two children with my husband prompts me to sometimes reflect on my BC (Before Children) life to help make sense of who I am now. Average or not, I have had defining moments that radically influenced who I am and shifted the trajectory I've been on. Healing from an eating disorder was a big one. Getting married to Arnold was another one. Having my first child, Aidan, and then my daughter, Aila, four and half years later, were two more. Defining moments, both positive and negative, are crucial components of our personal narratives. Perhaps we call them "defining" moments because they call us to rise to the occasion and be the person we will be proud of later. And even though defining moments differ wildly for everyone, they are an inevitable part of life, and they often mark the beginning of a distinct new phase. Those moments could be marriage, the death of a family member, bankruptcy, a new job or career change, a move to a new city, retirement, or graduating college, just to name a few. Everyone has moments, events, and situations that divide their life into meaningful chunks that add to their personal story of "me."

I'm particularly interested in the meaningful events that divide one's life into "old version of me" and "new version of me." That moment for me was becoming a mother for the first time. Giving birth to Aidan and taking on the permanent role of "mom" gifted me entirely new eyes to perceive through. While there was certainly the wonderment and awe of welcoming Aidan into the world, it was no simple thing. No words can describe the jarring displacement of identity I felt the moment he was born.

Up until that point, I had always considered myself spiritual—not viewing spirituality through the lens of organized religion, but through my fascination with consciousness and the nature of existence. Starting at a young age, I was enchanted with the big conversations about "who we are" and "why we're here." I remember finding myself in a psychology section in the public library when I was in fifth grade, stumbling upon *Being Peace*, a book about mindfulness by Thich Nhat Hanh, the (now widely known) Vietnamese Zen Master.[1] I loved that book. I then found many other books that satiated my growing hunger for truth. I read books from Jiddu Krishnamurti, Wayne Dyer, Louise Hay, Deepak Chopra, and other texts, like *A Course in Miracles* and the *Tao Te Ching*.[2]

That hunger to know deeply about the human mind and spirit, which has persisted from then until now, I believe is the reason for the extraordinary occurrence that profoundly changed me in an instant. It happened in my closet on a summer day in August of 2008—a day that marks the division between an "old version of me" and a "new version of me."

It was about 3:30 p.m. I had just arrived home from a one-hour meeting at the office where I worked in Silicon Valley. I normally hated going all the way down to the office for just one meeting, but this time I was too distracted to even notice the three and half hours spent in the car between San Francisco and Santa Clara and back again. On this day, I had requested a meeting with my beloved manager, Adrienne

---

1   Thich Nhat Hanh, *Being Peace* (Berkeley, CA: Parallax Press, 1987).

2   Helen Schucman, *A Course in Miracles* (New York: Viking: The Foundation for Inner Peace, 1976); Steven A. Mitchell, *Tao Te Ching: A New English Version* (New York: HarperCollins, 1989).

Whitmore, to discuss a life-altering decision that had taken me three months to make.

Adrienne was—and still is—one of my favorite people. She was the leader everyone wanted as their manager at Sun Microsystems. She was respected and adored by everyone who knew her; she was brilliant, kind, empowering, humble, and generous with her care and wisdom. Despite all this, I had requested the meeting to tell her I wouldn't be coming back to work. Instead of feeling energized for this new transition, I felt gutted and confused. It felt like a breakup of the worst kind, like the "It's not you, it's me" sort of thing. My doubt was all-consuming, trying to convince me I was making a wrong decision. My heart, however, knew it was exactly the decision I needed to make.

I was approaching the end of my three-month maternity leave after the birth of my first child, Aidan. Up until the day Aidan was born, my work—my identity as a professional—was absolutely *everything* to me. I had poured my heart and soul into that company for almost ten years. I was twenty-nine years old, extremely proud of the career I had established, determined to become an executive by forty. But now as a mom, it was all different. Aidan's birth threw me into a state of being absolutely nothing could have prepared me for. His birth, his presence in my life as a precious baby who I was now completely enamored with and responsible for, shook up everything I knew about myself. I had a runway of three months to figure out how to simultaneously be both *mom* and *aspiring executive*. I figured that three months would be enough time to bond with my child and successfully compartmentalize parenting and professional-ing. However, while those three months had been illuminating, I was far from the clarity I expected, especially given my familiarity with kids.

I'm the oldest daughter of three children—five and half years older than my sister, Kate, and eleven years older than my brother, Jake. My mom was devoted to us kids and made it a priority to be home with us while growing up. To supplement my dad's income, she operated a daycare in our home. Our house was almost always in a state of loving chaos. There was never a day when we didn't have a gaggle of kids under the care of my loving mom. To help her bring order to the chaos, I was usually by her side as her "right hand," as she often called me. I eagerly and dutifully took it upon myself to organize games and events like obstacle courses, treasure hunts, and talent shows, as well as change diapers, feed babies, and read at story time. My adolescence was spent helping my mom out with all those kids, and I think that's why caring for children feels like a part of my DNA. That's why I had no doubt in my mind that I'd ease right into motherhood without a hitch.

The reality was a far cry from what I had imagined. I wasn't eased into anything. It was more like being shot out of a cannon and ripped away from everything I thought I knew. Let me turn the table so you can see what I mean: up until that baby is born, your entire world revolves around you. You are the epicenter of an important, all-consuming, self-centered orbit. Not self-centered in a negative way, just an accurate descriptor for where your primary focus is. There's no way to truly appreciate your self-centered reality because there is nothing to compare it to—you're like a fish in water having no ability to conceive of the concept of water. Your self-centeredness is the only orbit you've known since birth. But the moment your baby comes, BOOM! The center of your orbit changes and is no longer around yourself but is now over *there*, around that baby. The epicenter of your universe and the lens through which everything is now perceived—the meaning of your entire life—is now all about the baby. This isn't a bad thing; it's a beautiful thing. And yet it's acutely different, and massively disorienting.

Pretty quickly I discovered the root of this disorientation.

It's not that you lose your "freedom" once you become a parent. You can enlist family members and friends to jump in and give you a break. With a few resources, you may be able to hire babysitters so you can go out for a coveted date night. As they get older you can arrange playdates at their friends' houses to give you time to do the stuff around the house you feel guilty for doing when you're parenting. So it isn't *freedom of action* that is usually the challenge. It's *freedom of thought* that disappears. With that baby now as the center of your orbit, your decisions and actions don't affect just you anymore; every one of them affects the baby who is now the epicenter of your entire world. You begin to think long, hard, and twice about *everything*: what neighborhood you live in, what activities you include your baby in, a trip on an airplane. Your mortality becomes a focal point because you're not just living for you, you're now living for the both of you. After baby, you discover that you're still free to do the things you enjoyed before baby; it's just that now you don't have the mental spaciousness you had before baby. Again, it's not a bad thing. It's just really different.

After Aidan's birth, my thoughts were immediately and involuntarily reorganized. Everything that made me "me" was now questioned. And I wasn't in a place of neutral self-reflection at the time. I didn't sit down with a journal and pen, light a candle, and go through a thoughtful inquiry: *Hmm, now that I am a mother, who am I and who do I want to be?* No, it was more like I instantaneously lost my center of gravity, like I had just gotten off a tire swing at the neighborhood playground, having been spun around and around in countless circles. My two feet were on the ground and I was trying to walk forward—which I knew in theory how to do—but right felt like left and up felt like down. Instead of the disorientation delighting me like it had as a kid, I was scared. When would I find my equilibrium? I wanted to plop down in the sand and wait until I came back into balance.

Quite unexpectedly, my new phase as "mother" had become my dark night of the soul. At this point, I had navigated three months of swirling doubts, emptiness, and sadness for a loss of something I couldn't name, all the while buoyed by the love I felt for my son and the pride I felt as a new family of three. The depth of my internal struggle was not obvious to the outside world. I was silently suffering but with no obvious reason why. "Maybe it was postpartum depression," is a response I've received a few times. Postpartum depression or not, there was a churning transformation happening beneath my conscious awareness. I was in completely unknown territory without a map. In a void. Maybe that's why they call it a dark night! And maybe, just maybe, postpartum depression is really a catch-all term the medical community uses to describe the predicament so many of us mothers find ourselves wrestling with because they can't name the struggles of our human spirit.

What complicated this painful passage was that I had every single reason to be absolutely in love with life. My upbringing was blessed. My mother and father, who are best friends, are still together after almost fifty years of marriage; they both have loved me and my siblings unconditionally from day one. Now I had a beautiful and healthy baby boy, the world's most supportive and amazing husband, a beautiful home in San Francisco, friends whom I adored, and the freedom to not have to work. That last bit was the hardest, and—I won't lie—painful to contend with. *How dare I carry on like this is such a big deal! Do you know how many parents would kill for this freedom to stay home with their child?* And now, here I was, having an internal hissy fit because I couldn't make sense of why I felt so empty for deciding not to go back to work. My self-judgment was at an all-time high, and the postpartum hormones had me pinging back and forth between bliss and despair like a pinball machine.

I reasoned that logic was my only way out of this confusion. In order to come to a firm decision to go back to work, I derived for myself a framework of stability to operate from. I decided that I only had to say "yes" to one of these parameters:

1. Were we financially dependent on my income?

2. Was my work my life's purpose, my calling, the reason I believed I was put here on earth?

3. Was my work my only outlet for social fulfillment?

None of these could I answer with a "yes." Therefore, I decided I couldn't go back. But my final decision couldn't rectify the feelings I had of the bottom dropping out. If I don't go back to work, I wondered, then what have I been working so damn hard for? The biggest question of all screamed: *Who the hell am I?*

These were the questions burning in my soul when I got back home from my meeting with Adrienne, although I'm sure I appeared to be calm and centered. *Nope, no fire here!*

Arnold greeted me with Aidan in his arms as I walked into the house. "So, how'd it go? How'd Adrienne take it?" he asked.

"Fine. Adrienne completely understood and was more gracious than I could have hoped. She's a mom herself."

"How are you feeling?"

"Fine. I think. It's the right thing to do. I'll be right back; I'm going to go change."

Walking up the stairs to our bedroom felt like walking in thick mud—heavy and mournful, like I was walking away from a part of myself forever. Walking up each step and into our bedroom marked the beginning of my new life as a stay-at-home mom. It was perplexing to be simultaneously excited about the new life I was walking into while mourning who I knew myself to be.

To inaugurate this transition was to do the only natural thing—to change from my work clothes into my mommy uniform, the yoga leggings and faded fifteen-year-old college sweatshirt with spit-up stains on it. But what I really wanted was to spend a moment in my closet. My closet was something of a sanctuary for me. Instead of getting brilliant insights in the shower or on long runs or hikes, like people often do, it was in my closet that many of my thoughtful reflections would emerge—and probably because this closet was no normal closet.

After Arnold asked me to move in with him, shortly after we started dating, he was determined to make more space for my stuff. Living in a Victorian, closets are pretty much a luxury. Lovingly committed to making me feel at home, he ingeniously converted the sunroom off our bedroom into a gorgeous walk-in closet. This sunroom, now closet, had access to the balcony overlooking a greenbelt spanning the luscious greenery of our neighbors' backyards on Clayton Street. My closet was walled with windows, allowing sunshine to filter through the one-way shades, providing the perfect lighting for thoughtful contemplation.

As I entered my favorite quiet place, I took a deep breath and softened my gaze as I peered out at the soothing greenery, settling me into a feeling of peace I hadn't felt yet that day.

Peace.

Then the internal dialogue emerged, the same silent interrogation that had been plaguing me for three months: *Why don't I feel peace about my decision to walk away from my career? Why do I not feel at peace about deciding to stay home and raise my child? Why do I feel like the bottom has dropped out? Why can't I make sense of anything in my life right now?*

What happened next I have no reasonable explanation for, except that it was born solely out of an impulse that was not directed by my conscious thoughts. Some part of me let my logical mind off the hook, and I surrendered my confusion over to something else, something bigger than me. My arms flew out and up to the ceiling. I looked up and appealed to something of unknown origin, "I give up. *You* show me the way."

The force within me that compelled those words to come out of my mouth is still a mystery. I have no idea what *you* I was referring to. I've always believed in something bigger than me but never in a traditional God-like way. For that reason, I had never prayed like that.

I consider myself to be spiritual but not institutionally religious. I'm extremely passionate about the intersection of science and spirituality, and I totally geek out on all kinds of existential conversations. The meaning of life. Consciousness studies. Eastern religious traditions like Buddhism and Taoism. But I've never had a real interest in exploring the meaning of life through the lens of organized religion. I had chosen to attend an all-girls Catholic high school not because I was interested in Catholicism, but because I believed the quality of education was better than the public high school I was zoned for in Sacramento. I learned a lot in those four years of high school, in both academics and religious studies, and have nothing but appreciation and respect for the essence of what religion is all about. All of this is to say that all my life I've been spiritually open, familiar with and nonresistant to religious frameworks, and deeply passionate about "truth."

So while I wasn't resistant, I was still shocked when my questions were immediately answered this time in my closet:

> You've been going about it all wrong.
> It's not about figuring it out,
> it's about feeling it out.

I didn't hear these words being spoken. Instead, the essence of this statement reverberated through every cell of my body, and I was injected with a *knowing* that I have no way of fully describing. It was like my perception was snapped into alignment, in the same way a chiropractor would align my spine with one strong adjustment. My disorientation was miraculously corrected in an instant.

It was a divine download.

Or at least that's how I refer to it. There is no amount of logic or reasoning that can explain what happened in that moment in my closet, and there's definitely no good explanation for what resulted. But it was this moment that changed me from a human being reaching for spirituality, to a spiritual being reaching toward humanity. And it was through no effort of my own; it just happened.

What I can tell you with certainty is that my agonizing confusion ended abruptly that summer day. I was unexpectedly hit with a powerful answer, catalyzing a spiritual metamorphosis and a 180-degree shift in my life's trajectory. It was the turning point from living by default to being always on purpose.

Now, I can't give you a one-sentence elevator pitch on what it means to be always on purpose. That's because while it's quite simple, it's also incredibly nuanced. It's you living your life *your way*. It's you living deliberately, passionately, and of your own free will—which is a reality that you must derive for yourself. And that's why I've written this book: to support you in becoming free of perceptions, beliefs, and patterns that may be in the way of living life more joyously and by your own design. Even if your life is already pretty fantastic, I want *even more* for you. I want you to wake up each morning excited to sink your teeth into life rather than feeling burdened by it.

After that hit of truth—*it's not about figuring it out, it's about feeling it out*—I understood that this thing called life is not that hard, and it's not that big of a deal. We make it a big deal. And we make it hard! In our hard-driving culture, struggling is our grand old tradition. We've been trained to fulfill the requirements, get the stuff, accomplish the things, and check off the boxes—and *then* we will be happy. Later. Not now. We've been conditioned to expect that if we follow the formula we will succeed and feel good, eventually.

The instant download revealed to me how that formula is profoundly misguided and flat-out incorrect. But what *is* correct is that we want to feel good. The insight—*it's not about figuring it out, it's about feeling it out*—hit me in my closet and opened the door to that Oz-like Technicolor world: I saw that there is a prismatic, vividly rich story of wanting to feel good. A multidimensional story. Everything we're up to, everything we attempt, everything we plan for, every goal we go after, everything we want, everything we think we want—it's all because we think it's going to make us feel better than we do. So at the end of the day it's not so much about the accomplishment, the status, or the stuff. *We want the feeling that we think we will have as a result of the stuff.*

What is the feeling that you most want to have? And can you see how it's the underlying driver for everything you do and don't do? (If you don't know what that feeling is at this very moment, it's OK! You will know very soon.)

Something about this book called to you. Maybe you want to have a major career shift, a relationship transformation, a healthier body, a life that provides you with both security *and* adventure, a deeper sense of peace and happiness, or something else of great importance—and whatever it is that you want feels elusive. Or maybe it feels damn near impossible from where you're currently standing. Maybe you're standing at a fork in the road and want to make sure you go in the right direction. Maybe you're in a time of big transition and want to get clear about what's next. It could be that your world has shifted on its axis like mine did when I became a mother for the first time, and you're right in the middle of your own dark night—feeling lost and forced to confront your attachments and compulsions, as I did.

Or maybe the word "purpose" drew you to these pages, which I have a suspicion is a code word that our souls know intimately—because no matter how far adrift we may believe we have gone from the person we were meant to be, that distance is only an illusion. You can't really distance yourself from the extraordinary human being you are—the one who has the courage and heart to be a part of this world.

Whatever it is that brought you to this page, know that your feelings are your GPS, leading you to everything you truly want—and that includes leading you back to yourself. And it is the shortest trip imaginable to get to where you want to be, because in reality, you're already there. You are already, always there. On time. And on purpose.

Now let's go deeper into how you can *feel* your way into the life you were born to live.

Chapter 2

FEEL IT OUT, DON'T FIGURE IT OUT

Our feelings are our most genuine paths to knowledge.

—AUDRE LOURDE, *CONVERSATIONS*

I may consider myself average, but I also consider myself blessed. As a life and executive coach, I have had countless profound and nourishing conversations with people from all kinds of backgrounds. While the nature of the coaching work varies wildly between clients, 100 percent of their aspirations boil down to one thing: they want to feel better than they do—more successful, fulfilled, free, happy, productive, clear, complete, or accomplished, for example. But it's not often they initially realize that a better feeling state is what they're ultimately after. They come to me because they want *something* to change. They are either not entirely clear about what needs to change, or they think they know what needs to change (or what they need to acquire, accomplish, or create), but they haven't figured out how to do it on their own. They want a coach to help make *change* happen.

You too want something to change so that you feel better than you do, otherwise you wouldn't be reading this book. The common denominator that threads through all the clients that have come through my practice, you who are reading this book, and me before my break-down/breakthrough is that it's *an improved feeling state that we all want*, not necessarily different life conditions. Some of us get that a change of job title, income, home, relationship, or any other outer circumstance doesn't necessarily guarantee genuine happiness at the end of the day, that moving the puzzle pieces around on the game board of our lives doesn't win us the deep joy we really want. Yet most of us continue to blindly assume it does.

The truth is, we're largely going about the game of life the wrong way. This is such an interesting phenomenon, because in so many ways we're well-equipped for success. We're trained to figure out—analyze, calculate, and strategize—the path to our goals, but here is the problem: we believe that reaching those goals equals happiness. We follow the formula and it leaves us scratching our heads, confused about why we feel empty, or astray, and we're left wondering how to fix it. Then we hit the realization that we *can't* figure that out and end up feeling hopelessly stuck, just like I did after Aidan was born. My head told me I wanted to be a devoted mother and an aspiring executive in the tech industry, that balancing both was my dream come true. Yet my heart beat for another reality—a completely different *feeling* reality—and I didn't understand how to make sense of my instinct. My "superpower" of mentally figuring it out was failing me.

Figuring it out not only stops working at some point, but it's also exactly the reason we find ourselves in this very real, very discouraging predicament. But why?

> Because everything you want, everything you think you
> want, everything you desire is not a thing at all. You want the
> feeling you believe those things are going to give you.

And right there is the crux of the problem we all share. We forget that what we're after is a feeling. We get so attached to the goals, forgetting that what we're looking for is a state of being or a feeling experience. We do everything we can to figure out how to achieve the goal—the "what"—and lose sight of the big *why*.

The superficial why is there: you want the satisfaction of achieving the thing. But why you *really* want the thing—the specific feeling state you think it will give you—is often not explicitly acknowledged or even known. Does anyone really stop and investigate what "feeling better" really means relative to the goal? When and where in our lives are we taught to do that? Not in school, usually not by our parents, and definitely not on the job. The standard equation typically looks like this:

Get good grades and you'll make your parents happy.
Get into a good college and you'll land a good job.
Get a high-paying job and you'll have a good life.

As you may have already discovered yourself, getting a decent-paying job doesn't necessarily equal a good life. More money doesn't necessarily mean more happiness. This is hard to believe, I know. Our instincts tell us if we make more money, we'll be happier. Why shouldn't it? More money means more resources to maximize opportunities for pleasure and more ways to avoid pain.

Interestingly, it doesn't pan out that way. Happiness researchers and economists have been attempting to find the correlation between money and happiness for decades. The disconcerting fact is that study after study proves there is no real relationship between more money and more happiness once you're above the poverty line. Case in point: a study on lottery winners showed that those who were surveyed a period of time after they won did not report to be any happier than their neighbors who hadn't won.[1]

So here we are. Despite the studies, we still long for the stuff and the status. And we dream of more money, thinking that's where the answer is. But let's break this down.

You say you want a new job that pays more money, but what do you think the money will provide you? Freedom? Peace of Mind? Pride? Possibility? Or maybe you say it's not the money, it's that you want a new job because you're unfulfilled in your current one. Stop and get clear: What is it you're *really* after? Money in the bank account means nothing until it invokes a feeling state within you. That's where the value is. And what is the value of a new job? Sure, it may be that you want to be doing a different set of actions with a different impact, asking different kinds of questions, and relating to people in different ways. But why? What will all that really provide you?

More to the point, this is a great time to ask yourself some revealing questions—questions that will uncover what you want to experience on a regular basis: What is the desired feeling all of this will unlock? Will you feel more stimulated? Will it put you more in touch with your significance? Maybe you'll feel more exhilarated and positively challenged. Or you may desire to have the experience of feeling both respected by your colleagues *and* emotionally connected to them. Or maybe greater autonomy and freedom is what you're hungry for. It's likely that a combination of these feeling experiences is important to you.

Consider all the big goals and wishes you've had in your life and ask yourself this question: *For what reason do/did I want this?* Inquire within until you reach a point where there is no answer other than a better feeling state. All you need to do is start with this super potent phrase: *I want . . .*

---

1   P. Brickman, D. Coates, and R. Janoff-Bulman, "Lottery Winners and Accident Victims: Is Happiness Relative?" *Journal of Personality and Social Psychology* 36, no. 8 (1978): 917–927.

The following examples are trails for you to follow *into your own answers*, the ones that feel good to you.

> *I want a good job (thing) . . . so I can live comfortably (feeling) . . . so I can feel secure (feeling) . . . so I can feel proud and accomplished (feeling) . . . so that I can ultimately feel good about myself and my life.*
>
> *I want more money (thing) . . . to cover debts and buy stuff I want (thing) . . . so I can have financial freedom (feeling) . . . so I can feel good about myself and my life.*
>
> *I want to lose weight (thing) . . . to reach my ideal body weight (thing) . . . so I can feel healthy to move and act in the world freely (feeling) . . . and fit into clothes (thing) . . . so I can feel proud of myself and my image (feeling) . . . so I can feel good about myself and my life.*
>
> *I want a relationship (thing) . . . to enjoy making plans with all my fun married friends (thing) . . . to feel wanted/adored/desired (feeling) . . . to feel fulfilled (feeling) . . . so I can feel better than I do when I'm alone (feeling) . . . because I want to feel good about myself and my life.*
>
> *And so on and so forth, until you get to something like . . .*
>
> *I want world peace (thing) . . . in order to observe and take part in beauty, love, and harmony (thing) . . . so I can feel safe and secure (feeling) . . . so I can have a sense that others feel safe and secure as well (feeling) . . . so I can enjoy life fully (feeling) . . . so I can feel at peace with all that is (feeling) . . . because I want to feel good about life on planet Earth.*

Every *thing* we want points to our desire to feel *good*. But we've all inherited a faulty map that usually stops at the "thing." In my case, I had achieved the stuff that was supposed to equal the perfect life:

✓ the prestigious degree

✓ from the prestigious university

✓ the awesome job in Silicon Valley

✓ the enviable relationship

✓ the lovely house

✓ the beautiful family

After my awakening, I saw the futility in my efforts to find ful-fillment by attaining more, different, or better "things." I even saw the futility of trying to figure out how to embody the life I was born to live. There was something I needed to explore before that life would be in reach. I was not who I thought I was, and if I wasn't my title or my accomplishments, then there was a *me* I had yet to discover.

Who am I? I wondered. There was no "figuring out" I could do to access that wisdom.

CHOICE #1: CHOOSE TO FEEL IT OUT, NOT FIGURE IT OUT

Waking up to the *feeling reality* beyond the thing we think we want is a big part of living on purpose. To be always on purpose is to be pri-marily guided by the feeling, and not the thing, because it's the most efficient, least resistant path to the ultimate end goal. Following the feeling, therefore, will never lead you astray.

Without really recognizing what it is we want to feel, how can we navigate in any direction at all? We've put so much importance on the middleman (aka, the outer goal) that we put all our effort into calcu-lating how to make it happen. This is usually done *despite* the cost to our desired feeling state, the inner goal, forgetting that this is the whole reason we set the outer goal in the first place! I'm reminded of the very common predicament fitness folks, like me, tend to fall into when it comes to the "last five pounds." We want to rid ourselves of those last five pounds because we believe the resulting change in physique will *finally* give us the pride, freedom, and peace of mind to enjoy life without constant self-criticism. But the effort required to remove those last five pounds and keep them off is anything but freeing and joyful. We want the thing (ideal body weight), assuming it's going to set us free from our own judgment, but in the effort of trying to attain the thing, we're not free at all. We choose the thing, forsaking the feeling we're really after in the first place.

Feel it out, don't figure it out. It's simultaneously obvious and scary. It sounds New-Agey and irresponsible. Why? Because we've trained ourselves away from trusting or even recognizing our feelings. Look, I know being told to "feel it out" may seem like a banal cop-out and most definitely not a derivation from a mathematically trained, hyper-rational coach. You should see the shock in my clients' faces when I suggest this as a replacement to their current modus operandi. "What? Follow my feeling? But what if it leads me down the wrong road? What if it makes no sense?"

Yes, follow your feeling. Look where calculated "sense" has gotten you. Are you sitting there resigned, unfulfilled and hollow in a job, relationship, or life situation that essentially checks off most of the boxes in the list of what a complete life contains? (Except for the most important one—the feeling in your body and soul that you're living the life you were born to live; that feeling that you are authentically and fully *you*.)

Think of it this way: If you were to truly follow your feeling, and honestly act on what is inspiring and life-giving, how could it lead you astray? How could it mislead you if what you're after is the best possible feeling state in the first place?

I'm not trying to convince you to give up your desire for stuff and throw all your effort to the wind—and then let the winds of impulse carry you. Not at all. Define enticing outer goals for yourself, ones you've actually sat down and mapped out as an obvious direct line to your inner goal, to exactly what you want to feel. You can use the "I want . . ." mapping examples as inspiration. Let "feeling," not "figuring," dominate. When you honestly and bravely use your desired feeling state to navigate life, not only will you achieve a steady and reliable feeling of unconditional fulfillment, appreciation, love, and joy, the *things* of your life usually do change as well.

Christina's story is a great example of what's possible when we make a priority of navigating from the direction of how we feel.

Many years back, Christina came to me for coaching because, in her words: "Something's missing. I want to figure out what I want." Christina shared that she had achieved an amazing life on paper. She was a successful financial advisor, had a loving relationship with her husband, and had all the creature comforts she set out to attain for herself. Yet she wanted something more but couldn't put her finger on what it was that was missing. Was it having children? Getting another dog? Getting promoted? Moving? She was content with her work, especially since it afforded her their lifestyle, but she realized that she was moving through life on autopilot. She wanted to identify the goal that would take her out of autopilot and into exuberant engagement with her life.

"Christina," I asked her, "when you go about your day, what gives you a flutter of aliveness? What gives you that feeling when you focus on it, read it, do it, or think about it—an energetic rush of relief, as if your breath was getting knocked *into* you?"

"No question about it. Animals. Mainly dogs."

"Animals, dogs. OK. What about them do you love? When you think about them and the presence they have in your life, how does it all make you *feel*?"

"Nurturing, caring, connected. Alive. There is something that just lights up in me when I read about them, think about them, or care for my own."

"Now think about your job. When do you experience these feelings of nurturing, caring, and connected in your role?"

"Funny, it's the only part of the job that I like—the nurturing, caring for, and being connected to my clients as people. Admittedly, it's the *only* thing that I really look forward to."

My goal was to help Christina see that what she wanted was more of *those* feelings in her life. She had been thinking she needed to *figure out* what to achieve, when in fact, she just needed someone to ask her what she wanted to feel, and what would be a direct line to that.

Over the next few months she created more opportunities with her colleagues and clients that allowed her to feel more nurturing, caring, and connected throughout her workday. She discovered that while it was a big improvement that resulted in a promotion and more positivity on a day-to-day basis, it wasn't filling the void.

We then explored beyond the bounds of her current situation. We took a nonlinear approach, looking forward and backward in a quest for those ideas, experiences, and feelings that evoked Christina's uncensored enthusiasm. Eventually she remembered a long-forgotten childhood dream of owning horses and training dogs, which then sparked the "impossible" idea of becoming a veterinarian.

"What a preposterous idea! This is the stuff of fairy tales! It's not at all the path I've taken so far, and it would take so much time and work!"

"But how does the thought of *that* work feel?"

Her body posture changed. She settled into her seat and leaned forward as if she was going to tell me a secret.

"Hmm. Amazing, honestly."

"So what's the problem here? When what you want to feel is *amazing* anyway?"

"Well, it's just not what I was supposed to do. I'd be giving up so much."

Imagine the sound of a scratching record here.

"Wait! What? You're not willing to give up what you *don't want* for what you *really want*? You'd be giving up the feeling of being in the 'void'—on autopilot—to live as the person you really are: nurturing, caring, connected, and happy among animals, which you've said allows you to feel your own heartbeat. OK, sure, you will be giving up an income you've been used to for a period of time. But remember, that money you're bringing in primarily buys 'stuff' and 'experiences' to fill the void of not feeling *amazing* in the first place."

As a loving and compassionate mirror, I reflected back her fear of letting go of a faulty map, the one that was the source of the void, and urged her to trust her passions, instincts, wisdom, strength, and resilience.

"And c'mon now, when have you ever not rocked whatever you put your mind, heart, and soul into?" I quipped with a good-natured smile.

She realized she was stuck in figuring-it-out mode. She had been battling the thought: *This isn't what a successful person does. Who in their right mind drops their successful career as a financial advisor and goes back to school in an entirely different industry?* She saw that she had to relinquish chasing the "right" idea and follow her feeling.

Good news: she did. Christina is now one incredibly joyful and fulfilled veterinarian, living happily with her husband and two children in Northern California.

And it doesn't stop there.

Another client, Jackson, longed to feel independent and unique. Mapping this discovery with his hobby of collecting unique dish towels, he left the tech industry and started an online linen company.

Adam didn't know what to do differently to feel better. After he claimed his desire for more creativity in his life and realized that he unknowingly shackled himself to the path he "should" be doing, he left his career in higher education and is living his dream as a photographer.

Helena was taught all her life to *not* trust her feelings, but to become what any good, successful girl *should* become (doctor, lawyer, engineer). When she learned that "figuring it out" had been holding her back from living as her own whole person, she quit her job as a lawyer and is now a communication coach.

Alexis embraced her dream of being a stand-up comedian and is doing it—writing and performing her own shows—after leaving her job at a top start-up. She was set free by the simple realization that there was no legitimate reason *not* to go for it.

In the case of each of my clients here, and countless others I've not mentioned, they stopped chasing an idea about what they *thought* would make them happy (their outer goal), and got super clear about what they wanted to feel (their inner goal). They've lived right into their wildest and most fulfilling dreams by using a feeling as their touchstone, their guide, and the end goal rather than an idea of what they were supposed to do.

This is possible for you too, if you commit to the first deliberate choice of an always-on-purpose life: *feel it out, don't figure it out*. Now let's talk about *how* to do that.

THE CHOICES CHECKLIST

Where we're at in the journey:

☐ **Choice #1**: Choose to feel it out, not figure it out

Chapter 3

INSPIRATION: THE DOORWAY TO EVERYTHING YOU REALLY WANT

Your visions will become clear only when you can look into your own
heart. Who looks outside dreams; who looks inside, awakes.

—CARL JUNG

My client Kara was having a reckoning. She sat in my cozy office chair looking more relaxed than I had ever seen her as she shared with me what was on her mind.

"For the longest time, my only purpose in life, the only end goal I recognized, was making money and being wealthy. In the recent past, though, I have come to feel like this is a bit unsatisfying. Not that I no longer like money, far from it, but I experience a type of emptiness when I think about the work I put in and what I have to show for it. Really, I think my core value is to contribute positively to society. I want what I do to make other people's lives materially better. If it doesn't, then why bother doing it."

Kara had begun to feel it out—to check the barometer of her work and her life as a whole. She had been pondering these questions for some time: *How does this sit with me? How do I really feel?* She was clearly relieved to be getting some answers.

You may be at the point where feeling it out seems right, but you may also be wondering, *How the heck do I do this? What does feeling it out look like in practice?*

To get started, I recommend that you first notice how you talk to yourself. For example, when you're in the midst of a dilemma and are having a hard time deciding what to do, begin to notice how you speak to yourself in the decision-making process. Writer and activist Rita Mae Brown said, "Language exerts a hidden power, like the moon on the tides." We live the effects of our thoughts and actions, but we don't often map how the medium of language influences those effects. How you speak to yourself—your choice of words—usually reveals how you're navigating any given moment, if you're figuring it out or feeling it out.

Figuring it out sounds like this:

"This option sounds like a good idea."
"This makes sense."
"After weighing the pros and the cons, I've decided _____."
"I've analyzed every angle and now think I should _____."
"I can't figure out any reasons why I shouldn't do this."

If your inner dialogue is intellectually oriented, meaning, you're using words like "think," "assess," "calculate," or "strategize," then chances are you're in the processing of *figuring* something out. Oftentimes, you can tell you're figuring it out because it feels like the locus of energy is literally in your head, with frenzied thoughts in your thinking mind that feels to be between your ears, and often there is little awareness of your body in those moments.

Feeling it out sounds like this:

"This feels right."

"Something feels off about this."

"My gut says _____."

"I've got an inner sense telling me that _____."

"I just got a hit on something."

"I feel lighter (or heavier) when I consider this option."

"This choice feels relieving."

"I feel better now that I've decided to _____."

If your internal dialogue is driven by your senses where you're likely to favor the word "feel" instead of "think," then often the words you use about your thinking will describe a felt experience or intuition that originates from your heart or your gut. It may even originate from your arms or hands. If you've ever been told to "drop into your body" during a meditation or yoga class, that "dropping in" is a moment to get in touch with the whole of yourself, including your body; it's about becoming receptive to an innate wisdom or felt perception that is chock-full of information.

Although there is nothing wrong with engaging your intellectual capacity for figuring things out with logic and reason, for the big decisions and major choice points, feeling it out and dropping into your inner wisdom is invaluable. That part of you is uniquely equipped to lead you to the most expansive and relieving options, which oftentimes offer the shortest path to your most joyous fulfillment. Plus, not all decisions in your life are big and critical, nor do many daily decisions require deep discernment. For the rather mundane day-to-day choices—like deciding to stop at the gas station to fill up the car now or before an errand tomorrow, or deciding between a green smoothie or a bowl of oatmeal for breakfast—simple reasoning will do us just fine. Taking care to plan and figure out your day as a practice can be a superpower in being efficient and productive. But for the more significant things—like deciding to accept a job offer, add to your family, or move to a different city—the wisdom of your body has a lot to offer you because it speaks to you through inspiration.

Inspiration is commonly defined as the process of being mentally stimulated to do or feel something, especially to do something creative. It's also been referred to as a sudden brilliant, creative, or timely idea. One thing we can all attest to is how good it feels to be inspired and, conversely, how miserable life can feel when we go for long stretches without it. Many of us walk around like zombies, tolerating mediocrity and lifelessness as the norm. We've learned to ignore our true impulses, or the voice of our spirit, because we were told that following our heart isn't the sensible thing to do. With enough of that kind of numbing out, Chardonnay becomes a stand-in for inspiration, and we're left wondering why we feel so hollow inside. Now, I'm in no way implying that inspiration can't sometimes *come* from Chardonnay; some of my best ideas flow as abundantly as the wine when I'm with my closest girlfriends! But if we don't wake up to the *feeling reality* that streams through us as an energy source to plug into, we can easily rely *only* on Chardonnay to feel better as a fleeting fix.

True inspiration is so much more than that. By thinking of inspiration as the doorway to who we *really* are, we begin to awaken to the white noise that lifelessness has become. We begin to honor a life-affirming pulse that transcends rational thought, a pulse that connects us to something deep within but also well beyond our sentient self. We begin to realize that inspiration is essential to our experience of *living*.

So let's take a deeper look at the inspiration that makes us feel more alive, more like ourselves, and more connected to everything around us.

Inspiration comes from the word "inspire." As a verb in Middle English, "inspire" was used to mean "to breathe life into, or put life or spirit into the human body." I believe that inspiration is nothing less than the language of the soul. It's a direct connection to who you really are and the life you are meant to realize, a communication flowing to you as a feeling originating from a felt perception deep within. As Steve Jobs once said, "Follow your heart and your intuition. They somehow already know what you truly want to become."

You know what happens when we follow our hearts and our intuition? We become less attached to our goals and get more creative in our definition and achievement of them. Goals morph from static things that *must* be achieved to dynamic signposts, guiding us in the direction of more fulfillment, joy, growth, and abundance. As we journey toward one of our signposts, our landscape inevitably changes, creating new horizons, perspectives, and clarity on how to course correct and where to throw the next signpost. We get hooked on *momentum*, not accomplishment, and all of a sudden, the phrase "The joy is in the journey and not the destination" takes on a whole new meaning. We don't get hooked on the momentum of creating by checking off items on our list of accomplishments and achievements. We get hooked on the momentum of navigating intentionally and deliberately—*on purpose*.

SYNCHRONICITY: ITS POWER AND PURPOSE IN YOUR LIFE

After my "feel it out" epiphany, my faulty map for happiness was exposed with so much clarity that I instantly made an agreement with myself that forever changed my life. It sounded something like this:

> *Those ideas, impulses, and inklings that feel amazing and expansive—that feel like a life-giving energy surge that seems to come out of nowhere— they must mean something. If I listen for them and commit to acting on them when they hit, then maybe that's the shortest route to the feeling state I'm really after. So feeling it out means I must honor those inklings and*

impulses as the breadcrumbs leading me to increased joy, purpose, meaning, and creative expression—to who I really am and the life I'm meant to live. Acting on them is clearly the path of least resistance to the feeling I'm ultimately wanting, even if it doesn't make logical sense in the moment. When inspiration hits, I will commit to trusting the feeling in my heart more than the strategy in my mind at that moment.

All of a sudden, listening and acting on inspiration—*feeling it out*—became a delightful game to play. Yes, really—a game! A game that is truly inspirational and now a chosen life practice for me.

Three Steps for Feeling It Out: A Process for Integrating Choice #1

The three-step process I share here offers a choice in perspective and guidance on when to take action and when not to—each one designed to put you right in the middle of the rich, joyous, and always-on-purpose life that is calling you.

Step 1: Accept the concept of synchronicity

Synchronicity is like a higher-ordered experience of coincidence—coincidence that is charged with meaning and purpose beyond that which is directly observable. Synchronicity implies that there is more to life than meets the eye. It suggests that underlying the seeming separation of everything and everyone in our sentient reality is a cosmic intelligence or consciousness that connects us all.

This idea of Kismet is not hard to consider when you look through an expanded lens of perception; once you zoom out of our time and space reality and recognize that there is no possible way our singular human point of view could ever comprehend the mystery of existence (in the same way that ants could never fathom how social media viral posts, like the ice bucket challenge, could compromise their habitats and influence their existence). There is stuff happening out there in the vastness of existence that we have absolutely no ability to understand. We tend to go through life believing that we're limited to our five primary senses. Which begs the question: What else might exist within this vast infinite universe that we're not able to perceive directly but experience the effects of?

Enter the phenomenon of happenstance occurrences—coincidences—like your cousin calling you *exactly* the moment you were randomly thinking of him on a Tuesday at 10:13 a.m. That could be considered a fun coincidence, for sure. But is it still coincidence when—after laughing with him about how "we're so connected!"—he shares an amusing story about his neighbor's crazy chickens? And this story about chickens sparks a small impulse in you to want this amazing "chicken little bird seed" scone made by a cafe down the street you've only visited twice? An hour later you can't stop thinking about this scone, so you decide to go get one for lunch. As you're in line in the cafe, you run into an old friend from college you haven't seen in twenty years! Wow! What a thrill it is to see this old friend of yours. As you're catching up and secretly marveling at this second delightful coincidence, you find out that he's the VP of sales for an up-and-coming start-up that just so happens to be in need of a keynote speaker for their sales kickoff in Las Vegas next month—and you happen to be an expert speaker on exactly the topic they want. He is beyond excited and relieved to have found the perfect match, and you are ecstatic about the opportunity. At 12:42 p.m. on a Tuesday in a cafe you rarely frequent, you end up securing a business deal that will be the highlight of your quarter. And it all started with the inspiration to catch up with your cousin.

Now is that *still* coincidence? You can see all the incredible connections to that one moment of coincidence. Crazy, isn't it? Think about the last time something like this happened to you, where it was just too uncanny to be considered coincidence.

This kind of magical-feeling situation is synchronicity. Synchronicity is coincidence with meaning, purpose, and momentum. Beyond our perceivable experience lives a world of energy and vibration, and within it a web of interconnectedness. While various spiritual traditions maintain a belief in the existence of an interdependent web of which we humans play a part, the web of interconnectedness is a foundational principle in Buddhism. In short, it is understood as "this is, because that is"—that the whole universe is a living, conscious, interconnected entity, and that nothing exists separate from this law of life. This web of interconnectedness provides the medium for those happenstance occurrences, the ones we often chalk up to coincidence. What I would ask you to consider is that what we usually think of as random or chance incidents are really signals from this invisible world of energy that are pointing you toward the life you are born to live. They fill you with a thrill because they are completely in alignment with the direction you are meant to go in and the intentions that you hold. In this way, synchronicity is a force connecting your intentions and your outcomes.

As you begin to see synchronicity as a phenomenon that is personally significant for you, it will add depth, dimension, and even fun to the experience of feeling it out. Synchronicity relies on your ability to *feel* in order to deliver its important messages; therefore, as you open to, understand, and embrace its power, you take a quantum leap toward your best life.

Research Points to a Web of Interconnectivity Based on Intention

Lynne McTaggart is an award-winning journalist and author of seven books, including *The Intention Experiment*, which highlights scientific evidence on the power of intention. In it, McTaggart details the collaborative work by the same name that she has spearheaded since 2007 with teams of scientists from prestigious universities and thousands of readers from more than one hundred countries. Their collective experiments have created the world's largest "global laboratory" to test, in some of the first controlled experiments, the power of mass intention.

What's the connection between intention and interconnectivity? In one series of experiments, for example, plants knew they were in danger and emitted an electrical discharge, signaling a stress response, the moment a researcher developed *the idea and intent* to burn one of its leaves—not when the flame got near the leaf. This and other experiments reveal the strong possibility of telepathic communication carrying on between every living thing and its environment. The experiments have raised the possibility that plants have a keen sensory inner life—with abilities common to animals, such as sensing, learning, and memory—and an interconnectivity with other plants and species, including human beings.

Beyond the findings with plants, *The Intention Experiment* has also shown that collective thoughts can make seeds grow faster, purify water, lower violence in war-torn areas or ghettos, and even heal patients with severe PTSD.[*]

---

[*] Lynne McTaggart, *The Intention Experiment: Using Your Thoughts to Change Your Life and the World* (New York: Simon & Schuster, 2007).

Step 2: Act on inspired thoughts

Do you know the single most effective tool for tapping into this cosmic consciousness of energy and vibration? Are you already sensing which one of your innate capacities helps you to know when to take action, when to pause, and what's in your best interest?

The answer is inspiration—the language of your soul.

Inspired thoughts—and the feeling of inspiration that accompany them—are those energetically expansive thoughts that when they arise you feel uplifted or, at the very least, hopeful. They are the thoughts that bring you closer to your ability to feel rather than scrambling your internal sensors or numbing you out altogether. They are the thoughts that often don't emerge from mental processing but instead feel like thought forms you get *hit* with, very much like that impulse to call your cousin at 10:13 a.m. on a Tuesday. Inspired thoughts feel light yet powerful, like an all-body knowing delivered with an energizing clarity.

Simply put, feeling it out is *listening for* those expansive feeling inspirations, impulses, and inklings, and then having a commitment to act on them. When you act on true inspiration, the result is seemingly effortless action because inspiration is your soul recognizing that—relative to who you really are, the intentions you hold, and the feeling state you really want—it's time to *go, go, go!* Act *now* because the right ideas are immediately available, the influential people you need to make things happen are right around the corner, and the books and other resources you've been looking for (but didn't know it) suddenly appear. The timing for every little thing you do is optimized. Inspiration is communication from You to you indicating that now is the time to put effort into motion.

When you choose to believe there is more to your experience than meets the eye (or more than meets the ear or skin!), then you are beginning to live your always-on-purpose life. This simple yet profound choice means you're saying to yourself, *Yes, I trust in the life that's being revealed to me.* Listening to, trusting, and acting on the inspiration that always accompanies synchronicity leads to greater unfoldment because inspiration is both the information and the messenger that runs through the threads of this interconnected web of reality. It connects you to the experiences and expressions that are authentically your own—sourced from who you really are—at exactly the most advantageous and delightful time, and in the most fulfilling way. These are some of the best feelings in life! Inspiration leads you to your greatest joy, meaning, and fulfillment. Inspiration leads you to the life you are meant to realize.

Step 3: Honor sluggishness

In the same way that inspiration is communication from You to you about the path of least resistance, lack of motivation is an equally important form of communication, and it must be honored as well. Instead of charging ahead with brute force, as we normally do in a figuring it out paradigm, your job is to honor this kind of feeling—where positive inspiration appears to be nowhere in sight—as a message from your soul to hold back. Viewing this through the lens of synchronicity, where it's possible that coincidental occurrences spring forth from a connected cosmic intelligence regardless of whether it can be explained by conventional mechanisms of causality or not, then waning motivation is crucial communication also. Sluggishness or lack of motivation, therefore, is not a symptom of laziness.

I repeat: sluggishness does not equal laziness!

Sluggishness means that on some level you are synchronistically resonant with who you really are and what you really want to feel, and therefore your impulse is inspiring you to hold back. Your wise inner being understands that in this moment you *could* engage, but the effort will not be worth the return. Again, that heavy or constricted feeling we typically call lack of motivation is a communication from You to you that now is not the time. So you can officially ease up on yourself the next time you feel this way. Honoring sluggishness as important information is a way for you to free up mental and emotional bandwidth, allowing space for inspiration to flow. That flow allows for a clarity about what you want to *feel*, above and beyond what you want to achieve.

This three-step process in *feeling it out* is honoring both experiences of inspiration and lack of motivation as real and as sacred. As a practice, it invites you to honor inspiration, however it arrives at your door, and never question your drive to do something that might appear illogical. Those out-of-nowhere feelings that light you up are messages that the inspired action is more than worth the effort and that synchronistic events and momentum will follow to confirm.

Reasons to Believe

Why should you believe all this? Well, those who have followed this always-on-purpose practice, myself included, have freed themselves from a faulty map and have manifested the life they were born to live. In my case, what I share is what happened immediately after I committed to feeling it out. It's wild, it's somewhat unbelievable, and totally real.

Within days of my closet incident, I acted on an urge to read physics books and rewatch two New-Agey movies I had gotten a big kick out of a few years earlier: *The Secret* and *What the Bleep Do We Know!?* Now, I'm not going to lie, they're both wonderfully corny, so I filtered out what didn't resonate for me and laser-focused in on what did, mainly excerpts from theoretical physicist Dr. Fred Alan Wolf and the inspirational author and speaker Esther Hicks. For the next few weeks

I dove into their respective books,[1] and I felt alive and buoyed by a force I can't explain. My impulses then guided me to read more books on physics by physicists Dr. Michio Kaku, and Dr. Robert Lanza and Bob Berman.[2] Then a choice point hit: I got the idea that all this excitement and energy meant that I was supposed to go back to school and get my graduate degree in physics.

Ah, yes! Now I get why I chose to earn my bachelor's in math, it makes perfect sense! I was apparently gearing up for this!

I called the department of physics at my alma mater, UC Berkeley, to discuss the plausibility of my idea, and although I was excited, I noticed that my head felt frenzied and my chest slightly constricted. As I continued to research my options in an advanced degree in physics and think through what my next steps would be over the coming weeks, these feelings and sensations persisted. I felt simultaneously excited and weighed down. While sitting at the dining room table with Aidan snuggled in my arms, I realized that I was back to *figuring it out*. The idea felt exciting in theory because it felt like the right, challenging, and sensible thing to do. Not to mention, another degree would be a nice feather in my cap.

But wait! What am I doing? This is exactly what got me into my conundrum in the first place!

As soon as I saw my effort for what it was, I dropped the idea. Back to square one: following my inspired feeling. I trusted that the answer was emerging, and it was OK that the answer wasn't an advanced degree

---

1   Fred Alan Wolf, *Matter into Feeling: A New Alchemy of Science and Spirit* (Needham, MA: Moment Point Press, 2002); Esther Hicks, *Ask and It Is Given* (Carlsbad, CA: Hay House, 2004).

2   Michio Kaku, *Parallel Worlds: A Journey Through Creation, Higher Dimensions, and the Future of the Cosmos* (New York: Doubleday, 2004); Robert Lanza and Bob Berman, *Biocentrism: How Life and Consciousness Are the Keys to Understanding the True Nature of the Universe* (Dallas: BenBella Books, 2009); Robert Lanza, "A New Theory of the Universe: Biocentrism Builds on Quantum Physics By Putting Life Into the Equation," *The American Scholar*, March 1, 2007, https://theamericanscholar.org/a-new-theory-of-the-universe/.

in physics. I continued to read from other physicists like Nassim Har-amein and Stephen Hawking. I listened to Abraham-Hicks recorded workshops on long lovely walks through Golden Gate Park with my sweet Aidan in the stroller. And I devoured any scientific publication that had the promise of validating my thought that consciousness was the missing unifying principle needed to make what had become known as the "theory of everything" work. I trusted my impulses, enjoyed how it made me feel, and trusted that it was all working out and emerging as it needed to.

During one of my mommy-Aidan walks one chilly San Fran-cisco summer day, I had an incredibly strong impulse to reach out and arrange a dinner date with my previous team lead, Sarah Marshall, who, like Adrienne, was also my everything. Sarah led the charge for our team, and although I reported to her functionally, Adrienne was the boss of us both. I loved them equally and the three of us had an extraordinary connection. (To this day, we are still thick as thieves.) Now, Sarah was and still is the fiercest female leader I know. Her presence is big and strong. She is tough, intimidating, kind (when she respects you), and nothing short of brilliant. Her no-nonsense leader-ship style polarized folks into either Team Sarah or Team Not-Sarah. I was definitely on Team Sarah.

Arnold agreed to watch Aidan so I could have a girls' night out. Sarah and I met for dinner a week later at one of the hottest restaurants in the Mission district of San Francisco. Over sexy cocktails and far too many appetizers, we dove into all topics transcendent, spiritual, and off-limits. Sarah confided in me that earlier *that* week, and for the first time, she had met with a spiritual teacher named Marta Maria, saying that it was life changing.

There it went . . . that accelerated heartbeat, that feeling.

A strong emotional pulse coursed through my body. *I needed to see Marta Maria too.*

I got her contact information from Sarah, and the following day I scheduled my first session with her a few weeks out. That day couldn't come fast enough.

Marta Maria's and my first mind-blowing session was so impactful that it led me to decide that she would become my teacher too. Our subsequent sessions were so illuminating that not only was she instrumental to my spiritual growth and self-awareness over the next few months, she immediately modeled a way of being in the world that I knew in my heart I was meant to do too.

But it all made absolutely no *sense!* I'm not clairvoyant; I can't see or read auras or other subtle energies, and I definitely don't know how to chant like she does. My tools, skills, and gifts look very different. But despite our massive differences, she represented a kind of calling I knew I was meant for. I just didn't know what that looked like or how I would even begin to figure that out—or feel it out, as the case may be.

No bother. There was nothing to figure out. I was committed to trusting the flow of inspired feeling. And as I continued to do so, things got pretty magical. A few months after my first session with Marta Maria, I nestled in on the couch to read *The Spiritual Universe* by Dr. Fred Alan Wolf while Aidan was napping.[3] Out of nowhere I had a powerful and consuming urge to look up Dr. Wolf online. *Huh, how funny. Here I am, reading his books, and I know nothing about him as a person.* I pulled up his website, learned that he lived on the East Coast, and instinctively clicked on the *Events* section. Up popped a listing of all his appearances and talks for the next six months.

Oh. My. God. Am I reading this right? I rubbed my eyes and double-checked my calendar. Dr. Fred Alan Wolf would be speaking at the Unitarian church a half mile from our house in San Francisco *that evening.* What?

---

3   Fred Alan Wolf, *The Spiritual Universe* (New York: Simon & Schuster, 1996).

Right then my stomach filled with butterflies and my insides felt the way Snoopy's happy dance looks. I delighted in the confirmation of this feeling-it-out business; these impulses were guiding me in the most incredible way. By feeling it out, positive changes were happening quickly.

I rekindled my passion for the intersection where science meets spirituality.

I averted an advanced-degree-in-physics path that made logical sense but wasn't right.

I heeded the call to meet with Sarah so she could connect me with the spiritual teacher I didn't know I needed.

And now this? I didn't make it to Dr. Wolf's talk that night but following the "I *must* do this" impulse, I did go to the next event he was scheduled to speak at a month later in San Rafael, California, at the Science and Nonduality Conference. Everything about that conference was a *hell yes!* There I reveled in subjects and speakers, made connections with like-minded individuals, and was introduced to a field I had never heard of called transpersonal psychology. After immediately acting on my impulses to learn more about this field, I knew in my bones I was meant to study it. A few months later I was accepted into the master's program at the Institute of Transpersonal Psychology (now known as Sofia University) in Palo Alto, California. It was exactly what I was meant to do, even though I had no clue as to what I would do with it, and even though I was a full-time mommy to my precious baby boy. I trusted that my inspired feeling was informing me that there was a reason to go forth and that the answer would continue to reveal itself.

Boy, did it.

This particular field of study was exactly what I didn't know I needed to balance my left-brained, analytically minded view of reality. Up to that point, my search for truth had been guided by the need for irrefutable proof through the language of mathematics, which according to most scientists, is the language of the universe. I didn't realize there was a whole other way to study, understand, and experience truth outside of the bounds of objectivity. Studying transpersonal psychology felt like I was practicing a form of perceptual gymnastics—the entire process flipped, twisted, and stretched me well beyond my comfort zone. The end result was that my master's degree rooted me solidly and flexibly on a balance beam of understanding, supported on one side with a linear and logical approach to reality, counterbalanced with a nonlinear and subjective search for truth on the other.

In the process of finishing my master's, despite the fact that I was a full-time mom and a wife to an incredibly busy restaurateur, I had never felt more connected, alive, energized, and *complete*. Anyone on the outside looking in would have said the load on my plate was insanely stressful. The feeling of what I was up to was anything but. I was feeling more receptive, engaged, and delighted with life than I had ever felt before.

This was also my state of being when I got wind of a certification being offered through my university called Transformational Life Coaching. That electric surge pulsed through my body again and I knew that it must be done. Coaching certification *had* to happen. And it did.

With a similar kind of flow and synchronicity, this is how I came to work at IDEO, one of Silicon Valley's early innovators; how I became a public speaking coach for a communications firm; and how I eventually came up with the name Always On Purpose for my business. It all happened in enchanting and sometimes unbelievable ways that still thrill me to this day.

Most people say stuff like this is luck. I call it always on purpose. Deciding to live always on purpose and be guided in this way has produced the most phenomenal life, the life I was *born* to live. This is what's possible for you too. If you choose to honestly listen to what you're feeling in a more present way and commit to acting on the expansive feeling impulses when they emerge, you'll be amazed by how life reveals itself to you.

Bills, Bathrooms, and Brute Force

But what about all those things that need to get done that you're not inspired to do? What about cleaning the bathroom, paying your credit card bill, and doing your laundry? How do you *feel* those out to completion?

I thought you'd never ask!

I have really good news. In the feeling it out paradigm, all this stuff gets done too. But not by brute force, usually. (More on brute force in a moment.) Inspired feelings will always guide you to do the things you're meant to do, and ultimately want to do. And you have to trust that they will.

Why?

Because who you *really* are and the life you are born to live is a unique-to-you expression of the best feelings possible—feelings such as peace, presence, freedom, joy, fulfillment, appreciation, vitality, clarity, and creative inspiration. Your inspired thoughts and feelings, therefore, will never guide you to actions that leave you feeling crappy—as in delinquent, rejected, diseased, imbalanced, anxious, or distraught. All combined, your inspired thoughts, feelings, and actions will never lead you to *not* pay your bills, ignore or treat others poorly, take horrible care of your mind and body, worry about things you can't control, or say or do anything that makes you feel bad.

Now sure, you may not be inspired to pay your bills on a Friday evening at 6:30 p.m. because you're eager to begin the weekend. Instead, maybe you're inspired to take advantage of the gorgeous sunset and decide to take a lovely walk to feel invigorated, peaceful, and connected. Or, you're inspired to get home as soon as possible, kick off your shoes, grab a bag of potato chips, and watch the game. No problem. Follow your inspiration. Trust that you'll receive a nudge to submit payment on time because your ultimate desired feeling state includes freedom and peace (which don't result from a bad credit score).

This is where listening becomes mission-critical—listening to yourself and your inner knowing. Listen for your own impulse, instinct, or whisper from your soul—and then wait a beat for its directive. The secret to having fun with this *feeling it out* business is to trust that the impulse *will* come, and when it does, you must act on it. Even if that means cleaning out your closet at 5:00 a.m. because some part of you woke you up with an impulse to do so just at that moment.

Now, this brings us back to brute force.

First of all, don't confuse inspired action with effortlessness. Yes, it is true that when you act from pure inspiration the process can *feel* effortless, but that doesn't mean it won't require any work. For example, you may be inspired to write a book. The idea of translating your life experience, stories, and wisdom for others to read and learn from might be the most energizing and life-giving thought imaginable! Yet despite this inspiration that lives within you, you could discover that you rarely or never feel inspired to sit down and start putting words on a page. The clear ideas and right words aren't available when you need them. Well, we've got a problem here, don't we?

Lots of us experience this kind of contradiction: we're inspired to create or achieve a certain outcome, but we're almost never inspired to do the work it takes to get there. For example, we might be inspired to be healthy, yet we're never inspired to exercise. We might be inspired to have an organized office, yet we never feel the impulse and energy to purge our file cabinets. We might be inspired to own our own business, but we're never inspired to take the necessary steps to become an entrepreneur. Many of the things we want to create or change in our lives take focused attention and continued action to produce a desired end result. Just as important as achieving the end result is the process on the way there, because your life isn't on hold until the end result. It's your life in each moment, and it's to be claimed in each moment!

Discernment is the art and skill that will help you to bridge the gap between tolerating and living. Listening for and acting on inspiration requires discernment. Are you moving forward with a particular plan because you *want* the result or because you feel you *should*?

This category of stuff that you're seldom ever inspired to do is almost always represented by the word "should."

"I *should* clean the bathroom."

"I *should* pay my credit card bill right now."

"I *should* do my laundry today."

We all have this idea in our head of how things should be. We fear that if we don't keep up with our *shoulds*, then things will fall through the cracks and we'll fail miserably. But guess what, there is no way things *should* be. The "should" construct is exactly what keeps us from thriving. And I'm about to make this abundantly clear.

THE CHOICES CHECKLIST

Where we're at in the journey:

- ☐ **Choice #1**: Choose to feel it out, not figure it out
    - ☐ **Process/exercise**: Three Steps for Feeling It Out: A Process for Integrating Choice #1 (page 50)

Chapter 4

I SHOULD YOU NOT

Out beyond the ideas of wrongdoing and right-doing,
there is a field. I'll meet you there.

—RUMI

"Amy, have I told you the advice I give to every bride?"

"No, I don't think this has ever come up in our conversations."

"I tell them, '*Don't ever let anyone should on you.*' When I was getting married, my mom went crazy, telling me everything I *should* be doing." She said this was the case until she finally said, "'Mom, please don't use the word *should* anymore. It's driving me mad. Instead, why don't you try, Have you thought of this . . . Have you considered that . . . You may like this . . .'"

My conversation with Meghan made me laugh. Meghan is vice president of a large tech company, and I do a lot of coaching work for her global team. While we were discussing two possible keynotes I would be delivering to the larger organization—one of the options being a presentation about the word "should"—she shared her personal connection to it, revealing that she very much appreciated the significance of this topic.

Most people have their own nuanced relationship to this funny little word and, whether they realize it or not, it's never positive. When I poll participants in any workshop and ask, "Think of the last time someone told you that you *should* do something—*You should try this diet out, you should call your mom and check in on her, you should go get your moles checked by a dermatologist*—regardless of their intention, how did it make you feel?" without fail I get barraged with answers like these:

"Stressed."

"Guilty."

"Lazy."

"Burdened."

"Heavy."

"Obligated."

And the energy in the room sinks to the floor as people recall all the times they've been "should" on.

Now of course, tone of voice matters tremendously here. Not always does "should" elicit that kind of negative reaction. If one of my best girlfriends yells from the backyard patio over to me in the kitchen, "Ames! You should grab that wine I brought for us on your way out here," I feel no sense of burden, guilt, or stress whatsoever. In fact, I'm *more* than delighted at the prospect. And think about the times you've been hit with an insight or inspiration and recall the inner dialogue that followed. I'll bet you had a *should*-thought precede an energizing idea. For example, imagine now that you're in the middle of a meditation—or in the zone during your morning run, or daydreaming in the shower—when all of a sudden you get hit with a powerful insight about how you and your colleague can solve a pressing client challenge you both have been stressing over. I'll bet your immediate thought would sound something like: "*Oh! I got it! I should call him right now and tell him!*" The use of "should" here is energizing. The word "should" in this example is also rather inconsequential and could easily be switched out with "Will! Must! Can't wait to!" Statements like these are almost always life-giving and inspired.

This kind of should energy is vastly different from, "I should stop eating so much cheese." Can you just feel the heaviness in that? This kind of should energy is riddled with sadness, self-judgment, guilt, and dread. Can you imagine anyone saying that statement in an energized way? "I can't *wait* to stop eating so much cheese!"

Umm, no.

You can see there is a distinction we must make between the two kinds of energy behind the word itself. If you use *should* in a positive way and could easily switch it out with "I will!" or "I must!" then keep going and don't think twice.

But if you think, feel, hear, or use the word "should" in a heavy, duty-bound way (and you know exactly the kind of heaviness I'm talking about), then get ready. We're about to dive into the unacknowledged vortex of negative emotion created by six letters clumped together intending to spur us into action.

THE WORST WORD EVER

I think "should" is the worst word in the English language. Contrary to unchecked popular opinion, it does more harm than good. Why? Not only does it usually make you feel less than great when you use it (or when someone uses it on you), it implies the existence of a reality that doesn't actually exist but *should*, and worse, a reality you aren't currently aligned with. That right there is the recipe for genuine suffering and misery:

Take the reality that exists, assume that it needs to be different for you to be happy, better, or good, and then let the disappointment that you're not there motivate you to do something about it.

No, thank you. That's not the kind of life I want to live, and that's not the *living-on-purpose* life I'm inviting you into. In the last two chapters, you learned how to *feel it out* using inspiration as your guide, and now it's time to take on the next deliberate choice of living on purpose. This is Choice #2: Choose to know that there is no way things—or you—should be. There is just the way things—and you—are. Period.

There is a way you *want* them, sure, but there is no *should* standard you were born to adhere to in order to live the good life. The word "should" implies a fixed reality, somewhere out there, that you're supposed to measure yourself against, and if you do, all will be well. But guess what? There is no separate *should* reality. There is no big book up in the sky called *The Big Book of Shoulds* that details every little thing you should be doing by when, and with whom, so that you're doing it "right." As teacher Esther Hicks has said: "There is a big mix out there, and there's lots of different things going on, and there is not one way that was intended to be the right way. Just like there's not one color or one flower or one vegetable or one fingerprint. There is not one that is to be the right one over all others. The variety is what fosters the creativity."

Claiming the life you were born to live does not mean finding and aligning to some imaginary ideal outside of yourself. What breaks my heart is that so many people plod through life with this assumption unchecked! Why? Because we grow up hearing our parents use "should" on themselves and on each other, and we become accustomed to the resulting drama. Then, we get used to them "should-ing" on us: "You should practice your piano. You should be spending more time on math. You should pick up your room without me reminding you." It becomes a natural part of the family dialogue, and we end up internalizing it as a way to get stuff done. After becoming desensitized to the discomfort "should" brings, we don't think to examine the reality that "should" really is—especially after we've become convinced that our successes are due, in large part, to all the should-ing we've done on ourselves.

Now, it may or may not be true that you've used a ton of shoulds and a lot of brute force to get you to the life you are living today. Wherever you are right now—and how you arrived there—is to be celebrated because, guess what, you've been doing the darn best you can with all that you've got. Truly. If you could have done better, you would have. And if you had known better, you'd have done better. And if you think that's not true, then you truly didn't know better!

THE POWER TO CHOOSE IS YOUR SUPERPOWER

Regardless of how you've navigated up to this point, we're now going to harness one of the most powerful forces in existence—and that force is *choice*. We're flipping the switch from autopilot now, moving from the default setting of should into an intentional and deliberate way of navigating through life. Choice is key here; it is *the* pivotal action step required for claiming the life you were born to live. Every idea, thought, and feeling you have rides on it. The power to choose what you become aware of, what to intentionally focus on, and how to direct and redirect thoughts, words, and actions is truly your superpower.

The first essential steps in exercising this superpower are (1) to examine your relationship to, and use of, the word "should," and then (2) to *choose* to navigate without it. The moment you realize that you've been holding yourself to some imaginary standard for no real reason other than habit, or fear, and decide to let this word go is the moment you awaken to the profound power of choice. Choosing to release yourself from the false construct of "should" is a huge step in claiming the life you were born to live. Not because you're rejecting the idea that there's a predetermined life you're supposed to find. Not at all. Rather, by listening for what truly inspires you and choosing *that*, you're actually honoring your inspiration. And you are literally creating what will be—moment by moment—from inspiration. Which is the same as claiming the life you were born to live, moment by moment! Why? By following the trail of what you *really* want, you experience the most freeing, relieving, enlivening, and life-giving feeling possible.

If your heart is skipping a beat at the thought of removing "should" from your life—either because you're excited to be relieved from its burden or because you're freaked out that you'll stop doing your laundry, eating your vegetables, or paying your bills—then I've got good news for you: you're on the verge of transformation. Get excited! Growing into new perspectives is exciting—even though it isn't always easy. No one ever said growth doesn't include growing pains. But these growing pains are wanted. They're the sensations that exist at the edge of your comfort zone, signaling powerful growth, not imminent failure. When it comes to removing "should"—and pivoting from "should" to "want"—you'll achieve more joy, freedom, and peace in your life.

DO YOU WANT TO CHANGE YOUR LIFE? REMOVE THE SHOULDS

"Shoulds" represent resistance, plain and simple. Teacher Esther Hicks affirms that with everything we want, there's an equally unwanted reality that we're avoiding. For example, if I want money, then I'm equally not wanting debt. If I want health, I'm equally not wanting physical pain or disease. In the simple act of should-ing something, a large part of my focus is funneled to the thing I'm pushing against, the negative consequences I'm trying to avoid.

In using "should," we may think we're motivated toward the thing we desire, but in reality we're faced the other way, in the direction of what we want to avoid, and the heaviness of what we're resisting dominates instead. That's why we feel heavy when "should" is in play. Should is the ultimate indicator that we're using resistance to get ahead.

Why is this crucial to understand? Well, imagine entering a 400-meter race with the expressed intention of winning. Would it serve you to put two-pound wrist weights around your arms and add a five-pound weight belt to your waist? No, because the energy required to maintain your momentum with the added weight would eat up the resources that you'd otherwise use for speed.

Unless you're weight training, resistance is *not* your friend. It's an anchor that keeps you from your own vibrant energy and mental agility. When you're in a state of resistance, you're compromising resources that fuel your creative cognitive and emotional presence. When you actively resist something—like how you look in that dress that used to fit perfectly last year, or how your boss gave you an overall rating of 3 out of 5 when you were expecting 4.5 on your performance review—you are using your thoughts and feelings to push against *what is*. In other words, resistance is an active exertion of mental and emotional effort against an aspect of current reality.

Sometimes it can be easy to catch when you're in a state of resistance. For example, think about a time you felt intense frustration with horrible commuter traffic on a weekday morning, especially after you calculated that you'd be showing up late to a *very* important meeting. That kind of acute stress signals that you're in resistance—the traffic is there, you're late, and so you resist it by wanting it to be something other than it is. Frustration is resistance: you're pushing against current reality, wanting it to be something it's not, and in that resisting you're just wasting energy. Is your frustration going to change the traffic? No. Is your anger at yourself for not leaving earlier going to make you arrive on time? No. Resistance is just an output of effort and energy in a direction that does absolutely nothing. It's futile—very much like pushing against your bedroom wall because you wish your room were bigger. Resistance doesn't work.

So in order to reclaim all the resources you may be wasting by pushing against what-is, you have to catch yourself in the act. But since resistance isn't always as obvious as pushing against commuter traffic, I offer you a sampling of the many sneaky ways it can show up:

- Procrastination. "I should be doing something other than what I'm doing."

- Any negative emotion, such as disappointment, annoyance, anger, or even boredom. "This should be different than it is!"

- Negative value-laden judgment of others. "They should be or act different!" "They shouldn't have done that!"

- Negative self-talk. "I should be or act different."

- Comparing yourself or your life to others in a way that makes you feel bad. "I should be farther along [more successful, more financially secure, more _____] than I am."

- Guilt, regret, or shame about anything that has happened in the past. "That shouldn't have happened." "I shouldn't have done that."

- Fearful thoughts about the future. "God forbid this should happen in the future!"

Each of these examples is an indicator of when we are pushing against current reality. However, I'd like for you to consider that these aren't just examples of resistance, they are *cues* that you're using the fear of negative consequences to motivate you into action. So instead of being hard on yourself when you catch yourself procrastinating, for example, get excited that you caught yourself pushing against what you don't want. Can you imagine having a whole new relationship to procrastination, where you're not down on yourself about it? Can you imagine not feeling regret about past decisions? That's all entirely possible, but it will take you understanding the common denominator that threads through all these examples: *resistance occurs any time you think, feel, hear, or say the word "should."* Should is the hallmark indicator that you are resisting what-is in some way. Contrary to popular opinion, that should-ing—that kind of pushing—doesn't facilitate change, it only wastes energy. The energy used to push keeps you from the inner resources that are designed to bring you the brilliant solutions you really want—resources such as creativity, innovation, and inspiration.

Bottom line: resistance squeezes out access to life-generating ideas. Resistance is a state of mental and emotional constriction that directly opposes creativity. Removing "should" removes resistance. When you remove resistance you access joy, freedom, vitality, and peace—all your birthright. And in doing so, you access the life you were born to live.

Let's dissect a common example of should-ing to see what's really going on. Let's take this much-revered and often-used statement:

"I should go work out."

Now, your noble self would *like* to think you're motivated in the direction of more health and vitality, but the simple fact that you're thinking, feeling, or saying "should" indicates that your focus is turned in the direction of what you want to avoid: exercise. What you're *really* thinking underneath the surface of that statement is: *I don't want to be fat*, or *I don't want to be weak and tired*. What you're not distinctly focused on is: *I want to feel energized! I want to feel flexible! I want to feel in tune with my body and appreciate all it does for me!* The use of *should* signals your desire to push away negative consequences (feeling pudgy in your swimsuit) more than you want to reach for what you *really* want (feeling strong and energized).

To understand this fully, imagine that everything you want—the stuff, the money, the relationships (and to be clear, it's the *feelings* these things would provide that you're seeking, so really it's freedom, possibility, love, belonging, satisfaction, appreciation, passion, etc.)—is over here, to one side of you:

Next, let's imagine that everything you *don't* want—like debt, rejection, humiliation, sadness, loneliness, disease, and pain—is to the other side of you.

UNWANTED:

- FAILURE
- JUDGMENT OF OTHERS
- REJECTION
- DEBT
- FEELING INCOMPETENT
- FEELING UNWORTHY
- LACK OF HEALTH
- MISSED OPPORTUNITIES
- ETC.

When you say, "I should go work out," you are turned in the direction of what you don't want, and you use resistance to push away from it. You push against your appearance, your weight, or your size to slog yourself to the gym. And sure, you might work out, but it's at the cost of feeling inspired. Why is this a cost? Because in the sheer act of pushing against, you are faced in the direction of everything you don't want to see, and you use force to push away from it. That force is a collection of thoughts, feelings, attitudes, and beliefs that are jamming up your bandwidth for inspiration to flow to you. Can anything positive come out of this? Maybe. But I'll guarantee you that the feeling of dread and procrastination is every part of you saying, *Sure, go ahead and proceed—but you'll never get the return you're hoping for, and it will not be commensurate to the effort invested.* In this state, weighed down by your shoulds, sure, you could drag yourself to the gym and restrict yourself from the things you love to eat. You could make some progress on your health journey. But would the progress be sustainable? And more importantly, without joy, is it worth it?

DISENGAGING AUTOPILOT

In making visible the true nature of "should" and its cost to your energy and your ability to recognize new possibilities, you are awakening to how you've been unknowingly holding yourself back. This awareness allows you to remember your superpower of *choice*. And I believe you are ready to claim this superpower because you are reading this book. So let's go! I'm now going to show you how to put choice into action to resolve this "should" predicament once and for all. With a simple perspective shift you will learn to disengage autopilot mode—living and navigating by default—to live on purpose instead.

To do this, you have two essential decisions to make. First, decide that this is a pivot you want to make. And then decide to use your feelings or mood as your guide. When you catch yourself in the midst of a "should," not only are you catching the words you're saying to yourself, but you're also catching how it *feels*. Notice that. What is the predominant emotion? Are there accompanying sensations in your body, such as tightness, numbness, or pain?

Anytime you think, hear, or use the word "should" and feel its energy present, that is your cue that your attention is turned the wrong way, and you're wasting your energy by pushing against things you don't want. The moment you catch "should" in your experience, immediately pivot to what you *do* want. So in this example, it might sound like this:

I should go work out. Oh, wait! "Should." No. There is no "should" here. So what is it that I want? Hmmm, I want to feel good. I want to feel proud in my skin. I want to be excited to put on my swimsuit this summer. I want to feel good. I want to feel energized!

As you've just done a full about-face, in your purview now is all the stuff that feels good, not the stuff you want to avoid. In releasing the resistance that was held together while you were should-ing on yourself, you've freed up your creative bandwidth for insights and ideas that were not available while you faced the other direction. With greater perspective and access to possibilities, ideas flood you that provide the path of least resistance to the feeling state you *really* want. So in other words, it might go like this:

Oh, yeah! I want to feel good! I want to feel energized . . . Wow, it's a beautiful day outside, I'm going to go for a hike! Oh! And I'm going to call my neighbor and see if she wants to join! It's been a while since we caught up . . .

This kind of generative ideating is not at all possible when you're solidly faced in the direction of what you don't want and unconsciously using your life force to oppose it. We have all experienced this myopia. With resistance we end up with tunnel vision thinking that the gym is our only option for not getting fat.

Here's another example of choice-filled inner dialogue:

Oh, wait! I want to feel healthy. I want to have a good relationship with my body. Hmmm. I stayed up until 2:00 a.m. last night finishing that report and I'm exhausted to the bone. I'm going to take care of myself, and instead of going to the gym and stressing myself out more, I'll go home, meditate, take a bubble bath, and go to bed by 8:00 p.m.

Health and vitality require an honoring of your well-being. If you're hell-bent on avoiding "getting fat," you'll miss the opportunities to create harmony within yourself.

Here's one more example:

OK, yeah, I used to say "should" a lot. But you know what? I do want to work out! Yeah! I want to feel good. I want to feel strong. I know I'll feel fantastic once I get going, and I'll be proud of myself when I finish tonight.

In this last example the action may be the same as if you went forth by should-ing on yourself, but the difference here is the energy with which you do it. Entering into action without resistance means you're more receptive to synchronicity, inspiration, and insight. By aligning your energy, your action, and what you really want to feel, you begin living on purpose—with intention and awareness—and your moments are flooded with joy and possibility.

By choosing to be deliberate about how you navigate, by choosing to care about the energy you bring to the table through all the thoughts you think and the words you say, you are stepping into the always-on-purpose life. By intentionally choosing to face in the direction of what you *really* want to *feel*, while using "should" as your cue to pivot, then you begin to claim the life you were born to live.

TRUST YOURSELF AND THRIVE

OK, now, tell the truth. Are you having thoughts like this? *If I don't operate from "should" then my whole life will go off the rails. I'll probably lose my job, I'll lose my friends, I won't reach my goals, I'll never get anything done, and I'll be a horrible citizen.* If so, I'm here to tell you that's not true.

Here's why: you have powerful and virtuous intentions, like wanting to pay bills on time and keep a good credit score, be successful and have enough money, generally feel good, and have a good life. Having set those intentions, then it would follow that inspiration—the language of your soul—is communication to connect your intentions with the inspired action at the right time.

Are you with me here? Good, because the implications here are truly exciting. This means that procrastination is an equally important feeling to listen to. Yep, important. From this point forward, I'm going to invite you into a whole new relationship to this thing called procrastination. When you are faced with an important choice and you choose to *feel it out* rather than *figure it out*, then just like sluggishness, procrastination is a signal for you to listen for the energy resulting from the focus you hold. Procrastination is valuable data to discern which direction you are facing! If you're procrastinating, I guarantee that you're turned toward everything you don't want and *should* is in play. So instead of being hard on yourself and assuming you're lazy, use procrastination as a sign to reorient yourself. Remember that there is no "should" reality you need to adhere to, and then pinpoint exactly what it is that you're pushing against. Once you nail it, do a 180 toward the reality and the feeling you *really* want.

Honor your procrastination, don't resist it. Trust the voice of your spirit. Trust yourself and what your mood is telling you. If "should" is in play, you'll know by how you feel (dread, anxiety, heaviness, fatigue, a general sense of "ugh"). Drop it and figure out what you *want*. It's in the *want*, the true desire, that inspiration can speak to you. When you're taking inspired action out of true desire, you've freed your creative bandwidth for flow. *Then* you have access to all those great ideas and the abundant energy to do the things that are continually pushed down your to-do list.

Four Steps to Freedom: A Process for Integrating Choice #2

Now that you've awakened to the hidden reality of *should*, harnessed choice as your superpower, and learned to pivot away from resistance and toward trusting yourself, here is a four-step process you can begin practicing today:

Step 1: Decide that choice is your superpower from this point forward and make it a daily priority. You get to choose how you navigate your life. You get to choose what you feel. You get to choose where you put your attention. You get to choose how you focus yourself into action.

Step 2: Every so often throughout your day, check in with yourself and tune in to how you feel. If you experience any bit of negative emotion (confusion, frustration, boredom, apathy, anger, fear, or another difficult emotion) then identify what you're should-ing. For example: *I should know what to do here. I shouldn't be fighting with my brother. I should be doing anything other than what I'm doing right now.* (Note: I absolutely guarantee you that under every negative emotion you have a *should* in play.)

Step 3: As soon as you've identified what you're should-ing—what you're resisting—then turn your attention instead to what you *really* want. *Crucial point*: Honesty is absolutely required here. Supposed failure is the consequence of choosing what you want in the moment over what you *really* want. Think about that for a second. *Supposed failure is choosing what you want in the moment over what you* really *want.* How many times have you been at that crossroads? Going back to the example of working out, you could easily assume that what you really want is to sit on the couch and pig out on tortilla chips, drink a half of a bottle of wine, and watch old reruns of

Seinfeld. This is where you have to be really honest with yourself. That may be what you want in that moment, but is that what you *really* want? If it is, go for it. But if you're getting a nudge from the wise part of you that's tapped into the truth of you, and you're getting that numbing out on tortilla chips is probably not your ultimate desired reality, then get quiet and still and identify what's underneath that urge. It may be that you decide that you want you want to feel relaxed and connected. With that insight you get the idea to go to that 7:00 p.m. restorative yoga class you really like with your girlfriend and catch up over a glass of wine afterward. But whatever the case may be, give yourself the chance to identify inspired action, and don't fall into the trap of replacing your true desired feeling state with a shortcut distraction. Be clear about your desired feeling—the one that lives where abundance and joy live. Change your *should* into whatever completes these sentences:

I want to _____.

I can't wait to _____.

I'm really excited by _____.

It gives me great relief to _____.

I would feel joy if I were to _____.

I must _____.

Step 4: Act. Boldly and courageously. Do what you want, not what you think you should. And *trust* that your inspiration will serve you at the right time all the time.

The reason these steps work so divinely well is because there is no rule book floating up in the clouds you need to pull down to measure yourself against. No one lives your unique life but you. No one but you can claim the life *you* were meant to live. No one can tell you how it's supposed to be for *you*. Be honest about what you want to feel and release yourself from fictitious ideas that keep you bound to a reality that doesn't exist. Try this on and I promise, the life you were born to live will go from a fantasy to a reality. *I should you not.*

THE CHOICES CHECKLIST

Where we're at in the journey:

- ☐ **Choice #1**: Choose to feel it out, not figure it out
  - ☐ **Process/exercise**: Three Steps for Feeling It Out: A Process for Integrating Choice #1 (page 50)
- ☐ **Choice #2**: Choose to know that there is no way things—or you—should be
  - ☐ **Process/exercise**: Four Steps to Freedom: A Process for Integrating Choice #2 (page 82)

Chapter 5

MANURE MAKES
BEAUTIFUL BLOSSOMS

Why wait for your future self to tell you how your shit turns out?

As a kid, I dreaded bedtime. Lying in my twin-sized bed in my small dark bedroom—taking what seemed like hours to fall asleep—was the most boring part of childhood. I can't, for the life of me, recall what my seven-year-old mind would have been so consumed with; I didn't have to pay bills or feed a family, I didn't have looming deadlines, and I'm pretty sure I wasn't preoccupied with worst-case scenarios about my future. My sole priority was to have fun and bedtime was anything but that. Lying quietly in darkness, I feared I might be missing out on whatever could be happening on the other side of my bedroom door: novelty, excitement, conversations, or laughter. I just wanted to be "up" all the time.

Darkness, silence, and stillness were together a necessity I couldn't appreciate then. I see it all very differently now.

TRAINING WHEELS, POLE VAULTERS, AND OPRAH

Reality is predicated on duality. You know this so intimately that you rarely think of it. You're swimming in duality, literally—from night into day, from winter into spring, through joy and sorrow, pain and relief. You discover early on that what goes up must come down, and that what is born will eventually die. Much to the chagrin of my seven-year-old self, I thankfully discovered that in order to be awake, I must also sleep. There is nothing in this universe that doesn't have an opposite or balancing force. This is the nature of duality. It's defined as an instance of opposition or contrast between two concepts or two aspects of something. Every facet of life is created by an interaction of opposites, or better yet, complementary forms, forces, or elements. But this kind of contrast that is duality isn't a "canceling out" (like combining 1 and −1); rather, it creates a stability or balance that allows for harmonious existence or function.

For example, do you remember learning to ride a bicycle? I do. Taking off the training wheels and being pushed by my dad as he ran behind me and my pale pink bicycle, accessorized with mylar handlebar streamers and a Strawberry Shortcake bicycle bell, is one of my most thrilling memories. In that big empty parking lot on a Saturday afternoon, I remember both the exhilaration of him believing in me and the terror of the inevitability of crashing onto the pavement. I anticipated a necessary teeter here and totter there in order to master the secret of balancing. In other words, I innately understood that to know what balance was, I had to experience what balance wasn't. And so I fell a few times—and fortunately not that hard—but just enough for me to file away a certain set of sensations that created the experience of "balance on a bicycle" in my brain.

If you've ever watched a baby learning to stand up, it's the same thing. To discover the muscles and balance necessary to take the unassisted bipedal position, they fall as many times as it takes so they know what standing up really is. Or consider the track and field event of pole vaulting. Pole vaulters know that to get really high on the ascent and clear the bar, they have to bow down as low as possible and unleash potential energy stored in that pole during the run. At any age and in any setting, in order to experience *anything* there needs to be an opposing force or aspect to provide the bounds of is-ness—to allow us to orient to it and feel it.

Not only is existence predicated on duality, but our very thriving is predicated on duality as well. Let me further explain.

The duality of night and day is accepted without question, and we eventually learn as adults that sleep is our friend. But when it comes to what we usually consider setbacks, we tend to have a big blind spot, especially because of our "don't worry, be happy" kind of culture. We usually make ourselves and each other feel horribly wrong for our mistakes, failures, and even our negative emotions. And for most human beings, death—what we perceive to be the great opposite of the life we know—is never easy to reckon with. Certain parts of our dualistic nature we accept, others can feel much harder.

But they don't have to.

If we accept the concept of gravity as easily as we accept that shadows are cast by the sun, then why do we push away the shadows of human nature? What if the shadows of our human experience—such as pain, loss, failure, or misfortune—are always on purpose? Not "on purpose" in a destined-to-be-unlucky kind of way, but as a powerfully meaningful and necessary component of growth and transcendence. The famous talk show host and inspirational thought leader Oprah Winfrey has been quoted as saying, "Where there is no struggle, there is no strength." Because of duality, the experience of what we don't want and who we think we are *not* allows us to become clear about what we do want and who we truly are. And the bigger the fall, the bigger the bounce—the more motivated we are to step into our most authentic shoes. If not for the contrast that duality provides, we would stay exactly where we are.

DARKNESS FALLS ACROSS THE LAND

When I was six years old, I made my parents regularly rent Michael Jackson's *Thriller* video on VHS. I would watch it on repeat, memorizing the lyrics and imitating the classic zombie dance that both terrified and thrilled me. I sometimes wonder if my intense fascination, almost obsession, with that video was a foreshadowing of what would be my future self. Little did I know that I would live into the lyrics predicting the hours around midnight when my future self would succumb to darkness.

Fast-forward to age nine. It was a typical Saturday of errands, chores, and housework. Mom cleaning bathrooms, Dad fixing something in the garage, and my little sister, Kate, and I up to who-knows-what. The TV in the living room was on, like it almost always was, with no one watching it. As I was running through the living room to get to the kitchen, I saw a scene on the TV that is forever burned in my memory. I stopped dead in my tracks as I looked on in morbid curiosity. A young girl, not much older than me at that time, was bending over a toilet and forcing herself to vomit. I couldn't look away. The shock and the horror of what I was witnessing was so engrossing that my eyes stayed glued to the screen. I slowly lowered onto the couch, and for the next twenty minutes I proceeded to watch this Hallmark special about a girl with bulimia. I was truly mortified. I watched her sit at the dining room table with her family, scarf down multiple plates of spaghetti, and secretly escape to the bathroom to vomit it all up. I got the gist of what was going on but scoffed at the absurdity of it: girl adopts weird behavior, parents don't like weird behavior, girl becomes addicted to weird behavior, girl comes to loathe weird behavior but can't stop, everyone is tortured.

My god, she's so stupid, I naively thought. *This is an easy fix, just stop!* I made my mind up that this show, and this girl, was silly and that it all made no sense. After those twenty minutes, I had had enough and innocently ran off to do something else, deciding, *Man, that would never happen to me. I would just stop.*

When I was fifteen years old, I fell into a severe eating disorder. It took me years to come to grips with this part of my past and share about it openly with others. Everything about its onset is imprinted in my memory. I vividly remember comparing myself to the other girls in my sophomore class, wondering why they seemed so secure and accepted. It appeared to me that they reveled in a kind of freedom that would only be accessible to me if I looked as "good" as them. Early on, I associated the popular girls' carefree nature and seeming joy with their skinny appearance, and I decided that to be accepted and feel that kind of freedom and belonging, I would have to be skinny too. Looking back at pictures, I'm saddened at how warped my perception was. When I look at old photos of myself, I see a healthy and active teenager. However, I was convinced that my build was too athletic, my legs were too bulky, and I didn't have the grace and coolness that the popular girls did. If I wanted to be happy, I figured I'd have to change the shape of my body to match the famous waif-like British model of the time, Kate Moss.

Then one day I snapped. I decided to do something about this fixation and end my suffering. I got a hold of the book *Take It Off! Keep It Off!* by Dr. Art Ulene[1] and consumed it over three days. I was forever changed by his idea that I could lose weight simply by chewing

---

1   Art Ulene, *Take It Off! Keep It Off!* (Berkeley, CA: Ulysses Press, 1994).

each bite of food thirty times before I swallowed. His book assured me
that by thoroughly breaking down the food by chewing in this way, I
would appreciate the food more, digest my nutrients better, and con-
sume much less in a period of twenty minutes—the time required for
the body to register satiation. Not only did it work, but it quickly set me
off on a massive control spiral. Each day as I practiced this, I became
increasingly fastidious and restricted my intake more and more. Before
I knew it, I was a bona fide anorexic.

This lasted for the next six years. However, over those six years my
disorder morphed into a cycle of anorexic by day, bulimic by night, along
with exercise to keep me going. Every day, my day started at 4:45 a.m.
to get to the gym by 5:00 a.m. I would work out at maximum capacity
on the elliptical trainer for at least ninety minutes, shower, then race
off to class and obsessively study all day, drinking nothing but coffee
and eating only apples and carrots. I would fall into bed by 11:00 p.m.
completely exhausted, relieved to shut my eyes but terrified for the part
of me that would emerge like a zombie from the grave.

At 2:00 a.m. I would be awakened by my starving body, and in a
semiconscious state, I would binge and purge in the kitchen for what
seemed like hours. Then I'd get up at 4:45 a.m. to do it all over again.

I have no way to describe the all-consuming hell that control by day
and out-of-control by night was for me. I was excellent at distracting
myself with obsessive, almost militant productivity during my waking
hours, but when I didn't have the capacity or willpower for control
during official sleeping hours, I would fall into the bowels of bulimia—
unable to climb out and oftentimes feeling that I wasn't much different
from someone helplessly addicted to heroin.

Just stop. Amy, please. Just stop.

God, I wished I knew how.

I honestly don't know how I did so well academically in high school
and college. I was gravely tortured by my thoughts and gripped with

an intense fear of food. I'm shocked that I had the internal resources to master mathematics enough to major in it at the University of California at Berkeley, one of the most rigorous universities in the United States. But despite the "Thriller" lyrics that haunted my subconscious, and my naïve nine-year-old self's disbelief in the power of addiction, I had another running belief that turned out to be more powerful than any of the distressing images I had absorbed—the dancing zombies or that young girl vomiting over a toilet. It was a belief my fifteen-year-old self grabbed hold of the moment I picked up Dr. Ulene's book: *I have a strong mind and god dammit, I'm going to do this!*

That belief, plus a series of other factors together, led to my path of healing starting at age twenty-one and lasted over the next six years. I give so much credit to my parents who, with their unconditional love and support, desperately provided resources to help me during high school and while I was away at college. They did everything they could to try to pull me from the abyss. My inability to heal before that time was not for their lack of trying. I firmly believe that I just wasn't ready. It wasn't until my best friend, Vinh—who loyally and joyfully studied math alongside me every day from mid-morning hours until I'd lovingly and anxiously kick her out of my apartment under the guise of "I'm exhausted, I must go to sleep"—made a move that changed the course of my life.

In those first four years at college I never opened up about my disorder, and Vinh never said a thing. All the times I would go off to the bathroom to purge any meal that wasn't sanctioned for my daily intake, she acted like she knew nothing. Looking back, that was honestly the most brilliant and loving thing she could have done. She knew that if she confronted me about it, I'd shut down and shut her out. She wasn't willing to take the risk because I wasn't ready.

In the early evening on November 13, 2001, Vinh sensed in me an opening. After walking out of our abstract geometry lecture together, she asked me to come to her apartment so she could cook us dinner. Now, the unspoken rule was we *never* went to her place; it was always mine. First off, I didn't have roommates, and my control-freak nature always handled cooking in the most outwardly gracious and generous way—where I would offer everything under the sun so that I wouldn't have to eat it. I wasn't willing to give that responsibility up to *anyone*. But she must have seen my sunken eyes and felt my broken spirit that early evening. I was frail, I was exhausted, I was shriveling up on the inside, and she knew it. Just as we were about to part at the street corner—where Vinh would walk to her campus apartment on Benvenue Avenue, and I would walk to my car to drive to my off-campus apartment on Lake Merritt in Oakland—she insisted I come over in a way she had never done in our entire friendship.

"Amy, *please*, just come over. I'll make us veggie spaghetti and you can show me your new laptop. *Please*. I won't take no for an answer."

After some back and forth, a part of my soul buckled. I agreed to come to her place this time.

As we ate her veggie spaghetti and drank her favorite Peachy Canyon zinfandel, she shared with me a secret.

"Amy, I have something to confess, I've been hiding something, and I feel just awful about it. And I need to tell you because I think it's a problem . . . I'm a smoker. I'm ashamed to say that I'm a full-blown smoker. I thought I just smoked recreationally, but I couldn't stop when I tried the other day. It scares me. The truth is, I smoke outside of Moses Hall after philosophy lectures, I smoke on my balcony, and when you go off to the gym in the afternoon for your second workout, I sneak in a cigarette. I thought I was in control of it, but I actually can't stop."

I was stunned. Here she was, my best friend in the entire world, and I had *no* idea. Tears streamed down my face—I knew and felt her suffering. I hugged her as she cried, and we sobbed for the collective pain we both felt in that moment. Her vulnerability was the necessary ingredient needed to dissolve away my rigid wall of secrecy and shame. That's when I felt safe to reveal my inner demon.

"Vinh, I have something to tell you too . . ."

Vinh listened as I shared my story between my sniffles and sobs, and after I finished, she looked at me with nothing but love in her eyes and said, "I know, honey. I know. And it's going to be OK."

Somehow, finally exhaling that night and putting words to my secret and shame took all their power away. For both of us. Vinh proudly quit smoking shortly after that evening, and for me, going home that night after our transformative release was like entering into a new reality.

For the *first* time since I was sixteen years old, I didn't fear going to bed that night.

For the first time in four years, I actually slept all night—through that 2:00 a.m. witching hour when my subconscious would nightly unleash the zombie, subjecting me to binge-and-purge hell. That morning, I woke up feeling a freedom I hadn't felt since I was a carefree kid.

If it wasn't for that evening, I don't know how my healing would have begun. And happily, I've never spent a lot of time thinking about that because it *did* begin. That year, in its right season, the behaviors of anorexia and bulimia fell away like dead leaves from an oak tree in autumn. And just as deciduous trees shed leaves for new growth, it took a few years to cultivate a healthy relationship with exercise and food. It took a little longer, starting at twenty-four, shortly after I married Arnold, to transform the mentality that an eating disorder is.

Perhaps loving and being loved is the greatest healer. Vinh and her emotional courage got things moving. And then came Arnold, ironically a San Francisco chef and restaurateur. I am indebted to him for his patience and understanding as he has been by my side, every step of the way.

RECKONING

While this is my story of darkness and pain, it is also my story of meta-morphosis. "Where there is no struggle, there is no strength." But in the midst of it, struggle was definitely more like unwanted hell. I remember moments when my eating disorder was so bad, I just wanted to end it all. There was a part of me that knew I wouldn't be an anorexic or bulimic forever, but the path from "here" to "there" was so elusive that I was continually subjected to defeat and helplessness. Entrenched in torture, I had no ability to consider my affliction as anything other than a nightmare. It felt like unwanted shit.

As I look back now, I see it as shit with a purpose—it was *manure*. My eating disorder was the contrast that fertilized my transcendence. It was my duality holding everything in place. Inside the intense experi-ence of struggling every day with a way of being that profoundly wasn't *me*, I experienced the sharp distinction of "wanted" and "unwanted." Living what I *didn't* want was a catalyst for powerfully realizing what I *did* want, the internal qualities that I value, study, and practice today— strength, resilience, power of reflection and belief, appreciation, presence, empathy, and always seeking a deeper understanding of human nature. I am certain that had I not fallen into the land of darkness from ages fifteen to twenty-one and worked to navigate my way out from twen-ty-one to twenty-seven, I would not be who I am today, nor practice the work that I do. I would not have discovered the true me and the life I was born to live.

Could it have been another way? Could I be living this authentic and joyful life had I not developed an eating disorder? The truth is, I'll never know. But the lesson here is, it happened. And I can't change that. What I can do is appreciate it for the gifts it has given me. There is no room for remorse or regret about any of the decisions I've made because I can say with *full* certainty that I was doing the damn best I could, with all that I had, in *every* moment. And if I could have done better, I would have. If I could have done differently, I would have. What I know *now*, is that I was always on purpose.

Choice #3: Choose to Know That It's Always Working Out for You

There isn't a human on the planet who doesn't go through their own experience of struggle that seeds their growth and transcendence of their particular perceived limitations. This is the nature of duality. To claim who we really are, we need to know who we are not. Are pain, fear, and suffering the only methods to grow and transcend? Of course not! We grow just as powerfully through love and joy. But let's not kid ourselves that we can create a life absent of all shadows. Where there is light, there is also darkness. As Esther Hicks teaches, "Contrast is inevitable." So let's not push it away. Let's choose to understand it and appreciate it for what it provides us. We can do that when we take on the third choice of an always-on-purpose life, and that is choosing to know that however odd, hard, or unideal life may be in any moment, it is always working out for you in the end.

Contrast is not shit, it's manure—the nourishing compost of our life experiences that can make beautiful blossoms of every hardship and pain we endure.

All of us have shit moments and none of us can change the past. So there is no point in pushing against it with judgment or resistance. We do, however, have the power to change our perception of what it means for our growth. When we shift our lens from resistance to appreciation, we see how life is always on purpose. This is what it means to thrive.

But it takes us actively composting shit to manure. It takes us bringing conscious awareness, honesty, discernment, and a ton of compassion to ourselves and all that we have gone through.

For me, composting shit sounds something like this:

Here I am, in present-day reality. I am married to my best friend, mother to the most incredible two children a parent could have, and appreciating the love and joy I experience on a daily basis. I'm able to look back at those thirteen years of suffering and without hesitation affirm that if it wasn't for that shitty experience back then, I wouldn't have learned my strength. I wouldn't have come to embody appreciation in the way I do now. I wouldn't have come to understand the nature of mind, habits, and behavior in the powerful way I do now. I wouldn't have developed the passion for empowerment and possibility had I not been given the reason to develop it. I wouldn't be loving, leading, and living on purpose in the way that I revel in now. My life would not be this, as it is, if it weren't for that. Seeing the shit as manure allows me to look back upon that darkness as fertilizer and feel nothing but gratitude now for that period in my life. I see it all through the eyes of meaning and purpose. In my now moment, I have nothing but reverence and love for the life I have lived, recognizing that, while it was incredibly hard, it was—and is—truly on purpose.

Many of us do this kind of reflection, where we're in our now moment and look back on our lives. We say, "Oh god, do you remember that boss? Ugh, she was the worst! But! If it wasn't for her, I wouldn't have been compelled to leave the company and discover my love of marine life and decide to go back to school. I probably would still be in the financial industry—resigned, tolerating mediocrity, and wondering where my real life is." Many of us can look back to periods in our life that at the time were unfavorable, but today we see how they served a meaningful purpose. What felt like shit then we innately see as manure now. That's what it means to compost it through the process of reflection.

Painting Forward: A Process for Integrating Choice #3

If we can compost shit looking backward, then why can't we do it in the other direction? Why wait for your future self to tell you how your shit turns out? Why not claim the purposefulness amid the shit and turn it into manure proactively? What I'm talking about is the process I call "painting forward." In the same way we look back and make sense of our mistakes, setbacks, or any form of darkness, and see how all of that has contributed to our current success today, we reorient our lens starting from now and project it toward our aspirational future self—actively converting pain to appreciation.

The painting forward process works like this:

Step 1: Whenever you find yourself in a shit moment or situation, stop and acknowledge that you're in a shit moment. For example: "I just got laid off." "I just discovered that my spouse cheated on me." "We're about to enter bankruptcy." Life is rife with shit moments, so if you decide to live always on purpose more often than not, just intend now to tune your awareness to acknowledge these moments for what they are: shit.

Step 2: Choose to stop tolerating the foul stench of unprocessed shit and make the decision to compost your internal conflicts right then and there.

Step 3: Pick a point in time in your imagined future. It could be two years from now, it could be five years from now, it could be ten. The point in time needs to be distanced enough from your now moment so that the essence of possibility emerges. In other words, three to six months from now might not be aspirational enough because it's easier to predict what might be true then. But two years from now, it's not as easy to anticipate what your reality will be. You can test this out. Think back two years ago to what you had predicted for yourself today. Were you accurate? Probably not. Once you find that future point in time that feels spacious, then conjure up a vision of what could be true that would just delight you. Did you finally start that business and are now a successful entrepreneur? Are you joyfully married with a family living in a beautiful house, perhaps with a white picket fence? Are you invigorated and surrounded by people who enthrall you? Paint a picture as specific as feels good and go no further, meaning *think as far as it feels good*. Add specifics only if it feels delightful. If your five-year vision begins to give you anxiety because you default to worrying how to make it happen, then don't add that much detail.

To be really good at this and to have fun, I recommend you identify what it is you want to be *feeling*, as much as what you want to be seeing. Imagine yourself embodying your desired feeling state at this future point in time.

Step 4: Come back to your now moment and reflect on the shit situation you're contending with. In the same way we look back to dark times in our lives and see how they benefited our future, and now current state, I want you to take full stock of today's shit situation and go the other way. Explain to yourself how this situation is totally and completely on purpose to get you to that two-, five-, or ten-year future state you envisioned. As you actively compost the shit to manure, paint forward a trajectory that uses this manure as a launching point to manifest that aspirational future. For example, in the case of being laid off, it might sound something like this: *OK, this sucks. All my dreams of climbing the ladder at the company I loved are shattered. But if it weren't for this forced time off, I wouldn't have the time or reason to look inward and discover who I really am and identify the fears that unknowingly hold me back. Maybe this is happening to give me* *the opportunity to grow from the inside out and achieve clarity on what I'm really meant to do in the world. Now that I think of it, I was on a path headed to nowhere, chasing after material gain and vain prestige, all the while sustaining a growing hollowness within me. Maybe this period of self-discovery takes me on a path of reading new books, signing up for classes, and learning things that truly invigorate me. Things like woodworking or hang gliding! And then, maybe, this is when I'll meet someone who reflects the same values and authenticity I anticipate embodying. And then, maybe, because I'm so fulfilled, my perception changes and I'm able to see opportunity where I wouldn't normally see it! Which could possibly mean I end up in an entirely new industry with a completely different kind of job where I'm not just successful, but I'm free and secure in who I am, and sharing this with someone I love. I'm glad I got laid off, actually. This is a launching point for finding true fulfillment!*

There is no right or wrong way to paint forward as long as it converts resistance to appreciation and pain into inspiration. All you need to do is creatively explain to yourself how this shit moment could be on purpose—how it's in your favor for your future state. All you need to do is consider shit as manure.

And this process isn't limited to the big stuff. You can do this with the little stuff and start to see the gift in everything. For example, *Gah! Where are my keys? I swear to god I just had them! And my phone? Shit, I'm so late for my appointment. Where did I put them?* Then ten minutes later you find both and think, *Shoot. I'm really late. But maybe it's because I'm avoiding an accident right now. Well, good! Then that means I'm really lucky!* Now is it true that you might be avoiding an accident? Who knows? Regardless of whether it's true or not, I'll guarantee that you will have a more pleasant drive and peaceful state of mind on your way to your appointment (and possibly avoid the *risk* of an accident by not recklessly rushing to shave off a minute or two). Choosing to paint forward like this is choosing to thrive, to enjoy, and to find purpose in your life moment by moment.

The painful parts of life, both big and small, don't have to be met with resistance. If we actively decide to honor duality and recognize that we grow from both pain and joy—in the same way a beautiful blossom needs both dark stinky soil *and* sunlight—we begin to live always on purpose. It's a skill to confront life's challenges, and the pain about *what's happening*, and convert that to curiosity and enthusiasm for *what will be*. It takes becoming intolerant of wallowing in pity, playing the victim, and seeing darkness as unwanted. It takes deciding that gratitude is better than blame. To live always on purpose requires you to take full responsibility for your life and, through your powers of knowing what you want to *feel*, compost the shit of life into the manure that allows beauty to blossom all over the place. That is easily done when you decide that it's always working out for you.

Remember: existence is predicated on duality, as is our ability to thrive. To know what you want, you have to know what you don't want. To claim who you really are, you have to experience who you aren't. *It's with this that we come to the topic of inner opposition: the necessary experience of living who you aren't so you can claim who you really are.* In the next chapter, you'll learn exactly what inner opposition is and discover how it's the internal mechanism that's *really* holding you back. (Warning: this understanding has been known to resolve long-standing patterns and set people free. Get ready.)

THE CHOICES CHECKLIST

Where we're at in the journey:

- ☐ **Choice #1**: Choose to feel it out, not figure it out
  - ☐ **Process/exercise**: Three Steps for Feeling It Out: A Process for Integrating Choice #1 (page 50)
- ☐ **Choice #2**: Choose to know that there is no way things—or you—should be
  - ☐ **Process/exercise**: Four Steps to Freedom: A Process for Integrating Choice #2 (page 82)
- ☐ **Choice #3**: Choose to know that it's always working out for you
  - ☐ **Process/exercise**: Painting Forward: A Process for Integrating Choice #3 (page 99)

Part II

DISCOVER THE LIFE
YOU WERE BORN TO LIVE

Chapter 6

INNER OPPOSITION: WHAT'S HOLDING YOU BACK

Let us be kind, one to another, for most of us are fighting a hard battle.
—IAN MACLAREN, *NEWS AND COURIER*
(CHARLESTON, SC), 1947

I waited to hear my name. My heart was pounding. It felt so surreal.

"Amy Eliza Martinez . . ."

For a moment, I had a split-second doubt that my name was really my name. Was there another "Amy" in the class? Irrational, considering there were only eighty others graduating with a math degree alongside me, and only about five other women at the time, too. But wait. I *was* the only Amy, right?

I walked across the vast stage of Zellerbach Hall. Blinded by stage lights, my sweaty hand grabbed the diploma. I can't remember much more of that scene; maybe it was the light. Maybe it was the adrenaline. But I do recall how my mind was screaming at me . . .

Is this really happening?

What if they find out?

I totally tricked them all into thinking I knew what I was doing.

I better grab this thing and get off stage before they catch on to me.

The "they" were in the audience: my parents, my grandmother, my boyfriend, my siblings, my friends. They were beaming with the pride I was half-feeling. I mirrored their smiles and enthusiasm, but instead of pure elation for the most anticipated day of my entire college career, I was fragmented by a combination of overwhelming relief and subtle bewilderment. Deep inside was an inner itch I couldn't scratch with reasoning. Despite my now official B.A. in mathematics from the University of California at Berkeley, I wasn't convinced I really deserved it. The proof in my hand made me a hero; the doubt in my head told me I was an imposter.

Yet I was *more than* aware of the amount of time, attention, and effort (or rather blood, sweat, and tears) that went into earning that degree. Did I love math? *Yes.* Was I able to do it? *Yes.* Was it easy? *No.* Did I do well? *Pretty much.* Did I believe myself to be a mathematician? *Yes.*

And no.

Have you ever heard of the imposter syndrome? Well, this is pretty much what it looks like. You may or may not have a story similar to mine, but I'll bet you're familiar with this inner tug-of-war. We all have this inner opposition that emerges, and oftentimes at pivotal moments in our lives—an inner critic or self-sabotaging voice that argues for our limitations instead of assuring us that we're already worthy. Even when we can look around and point out all the proof that validates our accomplishments or greatness, it's as if we can never accumulate exactly enough or find just the right kind of proof that gets us to an ultimate feeling of *completeness.*

I hear about this inner opposition from others all the time. I see the effects of it all around me, and I experience the inner tug-of-war myself. If you're human, then this inner opposition lives within you. It's something we all pick up in the process of growing up, while trying our best to navigate the increasing complexities of life and doing our best to belong.

Now, just so we're super clear about what we're all dealing with—universally, inside ourselves—let's deconstruct this experience of inner opposition. If you look up "opposition" in the dictionary, you'll get a description like this:

- to act against, provide resistance to, combat

- to stand in the way of; obstruct

- to set as an opponent or adversary

- to be hostile or adverse to; to set as an obstacle or hindrance

Inner opposition is the resistance you have with yourself; it's resistance to your worth, your competency, or your "enough-ness." It is self-doubt and a lack of faith or belief in your wholeness, completeness, resourcefulness, or resiliency. It's the energy of fear, either subtle or overt, that's generated when you secretly worry that you're a failure, that you don't really fit in, or that you don't measure up to others around you. Accompanying these limiting thoughts and beliefs are constricting emotions and an inner dialogue whose sole job is to keep you safe from failure and rejection. Its presence is as intrusive as wearing a life jacket in a bathtub.

And we can't escape it. It's called being human.

For each of us, the degree to which we experience this inner opposition varies greatly. The way it moves tends to be fluid, dynamic, and contextual. Meaning that depending on what's going on in our lives, the sabotaging inner critic is either a raging tornado or a sleeping dragon. For some of us, it runs our whole lives.

Many of my clients—who, by the way, are some of the most successful people in their industries—have poignantly described how this painful pattern shows up for them. Success doesn't guarantee escape from this phenomenon. As their verbatim statements illustrate, the voices of doubt and fear usually go something like this.

"I've always had it. Even as a kid. Even though I was an overachiever, I've always had this self-doubt. I remember as a kid, I used to worry about what people thought of me all the time. I don't know why; I grew up in a really loving household. Our parents expected a lot of us, but it always felt to me like they saw our full potential and wanted to support that. I've overcome many of my insecurities over the years, but that self-doubt is still there—and it weighs me down."

"If people really knew my background, and the issues and challenges I faced in my household, then they'd see how truly unsophisticated I am. Others would find out I'm not nearly as put together and 'worthy' as they think I am."

"Self-doubt feels like I'm constantly maintaining a heavy load. Almost like a drain in energy and bandwidth that could probably be used for a lot of other productive things at work and at home."

"Despite all my accomplishments, I still feel like I'm not good enough. I look out there at everyone else and they've all got it together, and I feel like I'm a fraud or an imposter."

"I'm terrified of being mediocre. I *have* to be exceptional in order to live a good life."

"When I'm speaking to my team, I'm completely clear, empowered, and effective. But as soon as I have to give a presentation to senior management, I seize up and feel like my words and ideas enter into a rock tumbler. I have a hard time spitting out what I'm trying to say in a compelling way."

"When I'm by myself or with my friends I feel just fine. But as soon as I'm around other professionals in my industry, I feel like an outsider. My inner dialogue takes over and hits the pause button on my personality and creativity, leaving me completely inarticulate."

"I'm very aware of how inadequate I feel around some people and not at all around others. It feels like I'm two people sometimes."

"I have this big dream of doing something great for the world, but who am I to actually do that?"

If any of this sounds eerily familiar and you recognize some of these statements as your own, then rest assured that you're in good company. We all have these fear-based narratives running amok in our heads. Sadly, they come at a high cost. It's hell to be at war with ourselves—not just because it doesn't feel good, but because it eats up valuable bandwidth and resources for thriving. If our internal dialogue—our thoughts—is primarily fear-based then we can't use those mental resources for creatively coming up with novel solutions to big problems, or discerning multiple points of view to connect with others in a compassionate way. If we're occupied by anxiety or uncertainty about our competency, then our awareness is channeled inward on what we think is wrong with us instead of looking out in the world and being able to focus on the things that we're appreciative of. Practicing appreciation is one of the most nourishing things we can do for ourselves, our well-being, and the world. Thriving requires that our attentional bandwidth is wide and free to gracefully and gratefully take in the things of life. Thriving means that we're thoughtfully allocating our thoughts and our awareness in the direction of bettering ourselves, others, and the world. That kind of focus and choice is not possible when there is a war raging inside us.

Think of it this way: imagine that I were to ask you to engage in a minor resistance training exercise right now. Imagine filling your favorite mug with water and holding it out to the side of you while you read this book.

For a few minutes, you'd probably hold the mug without too much effort while reading the next page. But wouldn't you agree that you'd be at least slightly distracted? Sure, you could follow the text well enough, but definitely not with the same focus you would have if you weren't holding the mug. After a while, the resistance would become fatiguing and then consuming. Your focus would be compromised, and your mental and physical resources would be channeled in the direction of keeping the mug outstretched and away from your original intention: to read.

This metaphor illustrates the effect of navigating life while sustaining inner opposition. Each of us metaphorically holds out a "mug" of personal resistance. To the degree that we entertain the dialogue of self-doubt, brokenness, fear, and limitations, we're equally wasting our life force—stealing from ourselves valuable energy and a greater bandwidth for creativity, compassion, innovation, and connection. Our bandwidth is our capacity to experience, express, and expand on these gifts. And it's ours and ours alone to protect and to utilize it to the max. And we *can* do this, *as long as we don't pick up that damn mug!*

What "mug"—what weighty inner opposition—might you be holding on to unnecessarily? What's keeping you from being fully present and available each day? Though each of us experiences internal resistance in varying degrees—sometime as toxic inner dialogue, and sometimes as self-sabotaging habits—I can guarantee you one thing: all inner opposition results from a primal quest for safety and an ultimate fear of rejection.

GETTING REAL ABOUT REJECTION

I've met with hundreds of clients over the years and from these interactions have been able to derive the common trends in what lights us up and what shuts us down. As human beings, we are drawn to feeling good; we are motivated by feelings of safety and security; afraid of judgment, failure, and rejection; and held back by fear. When I combine these trends with all of my research into the human experience—the body, the brain, the mind, and the paths toward self-actualization and enlightenment—I am left with a powerful realization: the quest for safety is more than a primal need; it is the basis for living a successful life, and—get ready for it—rejection is "death" to the brain.

Rejection is death to the brain? What?

If you're wondering how this may be true, consider this:

Fact #1: We're survival-brain dominant when we're born, meaning we're brought into this world with a biological directive to stay alive. The higher-ordered parts of the brain don't start developing until later. The prefrontal cortex (the most evolved part of our brain) doesn't start developing until adolescence and isn't fully formed until our mid-twenties. From the moment we are born until the day we die, our brains are constantly looking to keep us alive.

Fact #2: A human is entirely dependent on their caregiver for the first few years of life. When our mother gives birth to us, we don't immediately wiggle out of the doctor's hands and run down the hospital corridor looking for berries. We are entirely and helplessly dependent on our mom or another parent figure to keep us alive.

Fact #3: Rejection, as an internal experience, registers like pain in the brain. Thanks to scientists Naomi Eisenberger, Matthew Lieberman, and Kipling Williams and their 2003 research study,[1] we now

---

1   Naomi Eisenberger, Matthew D. Lieberman, and Kipling D. Williams, "Does Rejection Hurt? An FMRI Study of Social Exclusion," *Science* (October 10, 2003): 290–292.

know that rejection is experienced like physical pain, like an unwanted physical sensation, unlike any other emotional experience we have. Remember the very first time you weren't chosen for the team, weren't elected to student council, or when your best friend stopped talking to you for a reason you now don't remember? Notice how you talk about that experience to this day: "It *hurt* so much!" Rejection literally hurts.

Now, put these facts together and you'll see that rejection means something really big for humans. When we are born, our brain's top priority is to get Mom or our primary caregiver to fully accept us. If not, we won't survive. We are hardwired to feel that rejection could equal death. It's why we as newborn infants and our moms are flooded with the hormone oxytocin for bonding, why we practice the big eyes and smiles, and why we cry to ensure that Mom or our caregiver doesn't leave us for too long. When Mom has bought in to this role, environmental safety and basic needs, like food, water, and shelter, usually follow. Again, we do whatever we can to avoid being rejected.

Once we've weaned ourselves from Mom, that primal fear of rejection doesn't change much because, remember, rejection is like physical pain. Humans don't fare well in isolation, and some of the worst forms of corporal punishment have been (and still are) banishment from the tribe or solitary confinement.

We are all wired with a primal drive for belonging. Our well-being, and our very sanity, depends on it. Consider how this need determines the way you consciously and unconsciously navigate your day-to-day: how you perceive, how you operate, and how it may dictate the choices you make.

In the same way, the need to avoid rejection is another silent biological driver in your life—so much so that rejection is as triggering to your brain as a tiger chasing after you. The brain is equally trying to keep you safe both environmentally and socially. It can't differentiate between environmental threats (like tigers jumping out of bushes and people running after you with sharp knives) and social threats (like a humiliating comment from your spouse at a party or that big fat painful "no" you receive from someone you really like after asking them out on a date). Your brain is doing whatever it can to protect you from both.

Yes, rejection indeed feels like death to the brain.

Now you can see that it wasn't irrational of you to feel like you were dying after your first real heartbreak in high school. It's also not irrational to feel afraid of being vulnerable and to feel afraid of being turned down by someone you like. It's also the reason so many of us hate hearing the word "no" after making almost any kind of request. A primal fear of rejection is the reason why cold calling can be so traumatic for folks. In short, when you feel rejected it's completely normal to want to crawl under a rock and hide, quit your job, disappear, or just die. And because we all share this same quest to belong, it's also completely normal to do whatever we can to feel accepted.

ENTER INNER OPPOSITION

Inner opposition exists in each of us as a way to keep ourselves safe so that we're not rejected.

This is so important that I need to say it again: inner opposition exists in *each* of us as a way to keep ourselves safe from rejection.

Now, tying it all together, my inner opposition was kicking and screaming upon graduating from college when I became a bona fide mathematician. I was afraid of being found out. I was worried that I didn't truly deserve what I had just achieved. *What if others decided I didn't deserve it? What then?* A part of me was certain that I was precariously on the edge of being judged harshly and possibly seen as a failure. If the truth was uncovered, I would not be accepted. And I would therefore no longer belong. As dramatic as that sounds, in essence that is what we're all deathly—and unconsciously—afraid of.

Self-doubt, the ensuing imposter syndrome, and believing we're broken (or at least lacking in some way) keep us from putting ourselves out there so we don't get turned down, pushed away, and humiliated. Inner opposition keeps us from trying so we don't fail. Because if we fail, we're afraid we'll be judged poorly and shunned. If we think we'll be judged poorly, then we believe that we won't belong. That terrible outcome is just as triggering as someone approaching you in a dark alley in the middle of the night in a rough neighborhood.

Inner opposition is our brain's well-intended way of instructing our psyche to keep us safe from judgment, disapproval, humiliation, and ultimately rejection.

Now, depending on the degree to which inner opposition or self-doubt is present for you right now, there is probably a feeling in your body that you can sense. It might feel a bit like a hollow presence subtly occupying your mental and emotional space, like the feeling of someone reading a magazine article over your shoulder, keeping you from the fullness of your experience. Or, if self-doubt is accompanied by fear, then it could feel like a big anchor is weighing you down, like a boat in the sea, holding you back from your innate strength, joy, and brilliance, keeping you from being bold, vibrant, and free.

And here's the irony: whether it's a hollow presence or a big anchor for you right now (and maybe it's both), you probably sense that you are somehow doing this to yourself. You sense that it's an inside job. And worse, knowing you're responsible for it just adds to its weight.

It's maddening as hell.

Inner opposition—fear, self-doubt, feelings of inadequacy or lack—feels both familiar and fixable, and yet you can't quite get to the root of it. However, I'm going to suggest something to you now that we'll come back to later (because understanding this will set you free): on some deep level, you probably get that you have the choice of letting it go. Somewhere deep down you sense that you can *choose* to stop doubting yourself, let go of the fear of judgment, firmly believe in your enoughness, but you just don't know *how* to exercise that choice.

Choice does not feel like choice when you're caught in a pattern. And the pattern feels like a life sentence . . . and so you look for the key you think will finally release you. You look for some evidence to prove your worthiness, deservingness, and enough-ness. You try to win just enough approval, acceptance, and belonging to earn you the safe passage you long for. Yet despite all the efforts to prove your adequacy, with all the external validation you could amass, inner opposition continues to lurk in the background of your life, rearing its ugly head in certain situations, lying dormant in others.

If you were to get curious about the different expressions of your inner opposition, what would you find? What does your inner critic say to you? How does fear and self-doubt keep you from being bold, vulnerable, or fearless? What might your life be like without the weight of limiting beliefs?

THE CHOICES CHECKLIST

Where we're at in the journey:

- ☐ **Choice #1**: Choose to feel it out, not figure it out
    - ☐ **Process/exercise**: Three Steps for Feeling It Out: A Process for Integrating Choice #1 (page 50)
- ☐ **Choice #2**: Choose to know that there is no way things—or you—should be
    - ☐ **Process/exercise**: Four Steps to Freedom: A Process for Integrating Choice #2 (page 82)
- ☐ **Choice #3**: Choose to know that it's always working out for you
    - ☐ **Process/exercise**: Painting Forward: A Process for Integrating Choice #3 (page 99)

Chapter 7

WHAT THE HELL HAPPENED TO YOU?

There is no such thing as a "bad" response; there are only adaptive responses.

—DR. STEPHEN PORGES, *POCKET GUIDE
TO THE POLYVAGAL THEORY*

David's mom didn't read him a bedtime story in favor of attending to his crying newborn sister.

Jennifer's kindergarten teacher chastised her in front of the class for giving an incorrect answer.

Janna's older brother's friends laughed when he called her a "stupid baby who doesn't know anything."

My mom dropped me off at daycare for the very first time.

These are all very normal things that happen to us when we're growing up. Adults and other kids around us inevitably say and do things that hurt or wound us in some way, and usually without any malicious intent. Because we humans are a resilient bunch, we usually get through these sorts of things just fine.

Or do we?

On the one hand, these kinds of childhood scenarios are known to build our resiliency and give us the tools to weather adversity, manage harsh realities, and simply get along with others. We're all a testament to this. These early experiences also influence the development of our personalities, our strengths, and our values. And they influence the development of our beliefs—primarily our beliefs about *ourselves*.

You see, on the other hand, as trivial and as commonplace as these scenarios might seem, they can be defining moments that mark the onset of our inner opposition—our own internal holy war.

Like anyone else, it would be easy to blame my parents for certain limiting patterns and behaviors that have accompanied me through the years—such as doubts and fears that have stood in my way at times and the strategies I adopted to manage them. But that would be such a small way to perceive the big love that we share together. Instead of blaming them, I give them credit for doing the damn best they could with all that they had. I admit that I'm lucky because my parents are really wonderful people, and they're amazing parents. And despite them being amazing and loving me unconditionally, as a result of some of their decisions I ended up with inner opposition.

But it's not their fault. The story I'm about to tell you will make sense of what I mean.

However, before I share it, there's a guiding principle at the heart of my work that allows me to help people have massive breakthroughs, and that principle is this: no one is responsible for our suffering except ourselves. Yes, we do have an impact on one another, and every one of us is responsible for our own words and actions. However, no one is responsible for the suffering that sometimes comes from our own interpretation of events and circumstances. As we began to explore in chapter 5, shit happens. How we choose to interpret the shit and what we choose to believe about ourselves and the world is entirely up to us. How we choose to interpret the shit of life ultimately determines when and how we develop inner opposition.

As an adult who is devoted to growth and self-realization, it's this understanding that allowed me to find that gold inside the pain I experienced as a very young child.

My mom and dad have a great story. They met in Sacramento, California, in 1970, married in 1973, and in 1976 they took a leap of faith and together bought a nightclub. They were in their mid-twenties. They knew absolutely nothing of owning and operating a nightclub, but they did it anyway. They called it Bittercreek Tavern, and over the course of ten years it ended up being one of the hottest rock 'n' roll bars in Northern California. If we were to go back and do a study of why their bar was so successful, we would no doubt find it's because my parents were, and still are, best friends. They're both brilliant, loving, and extremely hard working and generous people. They have a deep respect for one another, and when the going gets tough, they find a way to laugh instead of argue.

In 1979, they decided to do what most young, loving, and devoted married couples normally do after a few years of marriage: they decided to have a baby. I entered the scene in October of that year. Turns out they were more than cut out for parenting. They were caring, completely devoted, and they ensured that I had everything I needed and more.

And they raised me in the nightclub.

I have nothing but wonderful memories of running back and forth from behind the bar, sitting on bar stools having conversations about god-only-knows-what with the old regulars, playing with the pinball machines, and belting out tunes from the stage in the early mornings while Dad was disinfecting the bathrooms and Mom was cleaning table tops and bar stools. I felt like the queen of my castle and could not have been happier.

Now, I consider myself to be *super* lucky to have been born to my mom and dad. I attribute my success and positive mindset to their parenting. Their ability to teach, empower, and love unconditionally has been my greatest blessing here on earth. I emphasize this to make a crucial point: regardless of the type of parenting you had—regardless of the unconditional love and support you did or did not receive as a child—inner opposition still happens. It happens because the fear of rejection is so deeply embedded in our psyches.

My inner opposition emerged at three years old.

It was an uneventful morning at Bittercreek. I was playing with my Tinkertoys near the propped-open front door allowing in a breeze to defuse the overpowering smell of Pine-Sol. I was immersed in a magical reality of wooden geometric shapes with my two imaginary friends, Lulu—who appeared in my mind's eye like Laura Ingalls from *The Little House on the Prairie*, and Laura—who I imagined identical to Goldilocks in *Shelley Duvall's Faerie Tale Theatre*. Completely content, happy, and consumed in a whimsical conversation with Laura about what Tinkertoys she was allocated, I looked up to see my mom looking down at me with masked concern.

"Clean up your toys, honey. We've got to get going."

"OK!" *Where were we going to go?* I wondered with anticipation.

I loved going places with my mom. I just loved being *with* my mom. My mom was my everything. I absolutely adored my dad too, but I *needed* my mom. I enjoyed being by her side every second of every day. We did everything together, and that's just how I wanted it—regardless of whether we were getting groceries, making a deposit at the bank, or browsing garage sales early on a Saturday morning. When I was with my mom, my world was complete.

She strapped me into my car seat in our gold Honda Civic, and we drove to a building that had a colorful sign out front. She parked the car, pulled me out of my seat, and I settled in on her left hip as she carried me into a place we had never been before. As we entered through the front door, my head spun from the dizzying scene of colors, patterns, and shapes on the walls and the cacophony of sounds coming from unfamiliar toys and children.

Children!

Other than my cousins, I had never been around other children. I was aghast with terror to see so many tiny people in such a small space. Within a few seconds of taking in the collective chaos of their unpredictable energy and high-pitched sounds, I felt uncertain and scared in a way I had never known. I welled up with tears and clutched on to my mom for dear life, wondering what we were doing in such a scary place. My innocent three-year-old thoughts silently pleaded: *Let's get out of here! Please!* I longed for my mom to turn around and immediately drive us back "home"—to our bar where I felt safe with my well-mannered adult friends.

I hid my face in her neck hoping that no one could see me if I couldn't see them. Muddled conversation occurred between my mom and a big woman next to her. Then it happened. My mom began to peel me from her torso and hand me over to the stranger she had been talking to. I screamed, I cried, I struggled with all my might to stay attached. My desperate efforts failed. I was now in the large soft arms of a woman who smelled like Play-Doh. I reached for my mom in a panic, screaming, while I watched her walk away and leave the building.

Gutted, empty, and feeling completely rejected, I formed a decision right then about myself in order to make sense of what just happened: *I'm a burden.*

To my young mind, this had to be true. I must be a burden and not good enough for my mom to want me around.

This involuntary decision was a self-oriented belief I instantly claimed to make sense of the terror-invoking rejection that all parts of my wiring were so deathly afraid of. Now, this belief wasn't an intellectual imprint, an idea that took shape in words. I was too young to map words to my feelings. I imprinted a *feeling identity* of "burden" so I could make sense of why this happened and ultimately protect myself from further rejection henceforth (more on this in chapter 9). This critical decision, this belief, was the origin of my inner opposition. This belief became, in an instant, a primary lens through which I perceived and navigated my life for the next twenty-seven years.

To further clarify the far-reaching impact of what took place, let's zoom out on that day my mom dropped me off at daycare for the first time and put together a few crucial data points:

1. My mom's biological directive was to care for me in the best possible way. Her very rational, and probably accurate, reasoning was that I needed to be in an environment that was best for a three-year-old—that I needed to be around children my age, playing with age-appropriate toys, and learning to share with other three-year-olds (especially because she was concerned that all I had were my imaginary friends, "Lulu" and "Laura," to play with on a daily basis). Her decision to take me to daycare was born out of an all-consuming love and concern for my growth and well-being. She reasoned that I would thrive if my days were spent with other (real) children in a daycare, not with adults in a bar.

2. A child's brain is hardwired to stay safe by seeking belonging and avoiding rejection at all costs. As a three-year-old, my biological directive was to stay safe by being at my mom's side at

all times. The terror of rejection I felt when my mom left me in the care of a stranger that day wasn't just painful, it catalyzed a survival response that had me imprint a belief that *I'm a burden* in order to make sense of what happened.

3. Our brains are constantly doing whatever they can to keep us safe, both environmentally (like keeping us from hot stoves and sharp knives) and socially (like avoiding rejection from Mom). We uniquely interpret our reality to ultimately stay safe. What one person perceives as threatening may not be threatening to another. Daycare doesn't objectively cause inner opposition; it's just that I perceived this particular event as a significant threat to my own survival.

For me, being dropped off at daycare was the first and probably most significant defining moment of my entire life. Why? Because the feeling I felt in my gut after my mom left the building is my first feeling-based memory of rejection. I have so few memories of my childhood and even less of my childhood before age five, but this event I remember as vividly as I remember what I had for breakfast this morning. The types of experiences that persist into adult memory with this kind of detail suggest that they had a significant role in shaping who we have become. It is the significant events and situations of perceived rejection that profoundly influence the beliefs we adopt about ourselves and the world. And these are the beliefs we operate from unconsciously until we choose otherwise.

Now, for any parent who may be reading this and freaking out right now, let's talk about daycare for a moment. Most parents would agree that the act of taking our children to daycare is one of the most normal experiences we can have as caregivers who either work or need a break. As I said earlier, it's not a truth that dropping your kid off at a daycare would cause their inner opposition, it's just that *my* brain decided that this particular event in that moment was as triggering and threatening as a tiger lunging at me from a bush. Daycare could have very well been your happy place from day one, and being dropped off there sparked happiness, growth, social learning, friendship, and creativity. Instead, maybe your wounding moment was that you didn't get an ice cream cone one summer day in 1985, but your sister did, or your second-grade teacher said something that deeply embarrassed you in front of the class. As parents, as children of our own parents, as siblings, or as friends, we're doing the best we can with all that we have. It's the dubiously exceptional case that someone wakes up in the morning with an expressed wish to really screw someone over or be evil. In fact, I don't think any person on the planet gets out of bed thinking, *I genuinely want to crush [insert name here]'s self-esteem and cause them to doubt themselves for the rest of their life.*

I truly believe we're doing the best we can, and when we genuinely know better, we try to do better. In the process of trying to do our best—in growing up, getting along, and working alongside others—we're inevitably going to step on toes and make decisions that may be perceived as threatening to others. We can't control how anyone will intercept and interpret the events of life; we can only decide to do our best.

And now that you're familiar with this idea that everyone just wants to feel safe and to belong, you can take extra care—knowing that underneath every single person's words and actions is a human being who just wants to be wanted, to be loved, and to avoid being rejected. With that awareness you can intentionally mind that primal need and, again, do the best you can with all you have. Awareness at this level equals compassion and empathy for ourselves and others. It's us paying attention out of care and love. When we bring this awareness into focus more often, we can't help but be inspired to do the best we can at every moment.

Every one of us has our pivotal, defining moments when faced with perceived significant rejection, particularly in the young years when our brain development is in hyper-growth mode and our reasoning abilities are undeveloped. We find ourselves in well-meaning, rather ordinary, and possibly insignificant situations that become truly life-altering because of how our child-brains make sense of the event. This isn't to say that it can't happen when we're older; it most surely can. Anyone who has been hurt by infidelity can attest to just how life-altering that can be—and not just because your outer circumstances may change, but because of the beliefs you consequently solidify about yourself and others to protect yourself from future pain. For the purposes of understanding the origin of your inner opposition, it's helpful to realize that it's more likely to happen as a very young child when the part of the brain capable of perspective and logic is underdeveloped and can't rationally make sense of complex situations like an adult brain can.

WHEN DID IT HAPPEN?

In all my thousands of conversations with clients, from all kinds of backgrounds and socio-economic environments, I have not met one person who didn't have some form of inner opposition. To revisit some of its most common faces, it shows up as self-doubt, self-judgment, social anxiety, perfectionism, people-pleasing, fear of failure, or a fear of being found out. Yet almost everyone I have worked with assumes they suffer with this reality alone. Despite their worldliness and wisdom, somewhere deep inside they feel that they are the exception, they're the only one who bears this inner opposition and everyone else is free of it. This kind of erroneous assumption—that it isn't true for others but it is true for me—is known as *pluralistic ignorance*. In silent suffering, and without full investigation into the truth of you, it's easy to assume you were born faulty and that inner opposition is just the natural consequence.

But that couldn't be further from the truth!

I'm *certain* that not one of us is born broken. Period.

Think of a two-year-old baby you've seen or held before, either your own child, a sibling, a niece or a nephew, or a friend's baby. Did you look at that small child and assume that they were anything other than *whole* and *complete*? Did you see inadequacy, incompetency, or the potential for brokenness in that innocent child? Did you suppose that that toddler had an opinion or belief about itself as being anything other than whole and complete? As much as that baby could perceive itself separate from Mom, did you believe any bit of their self-perception had to do with *lack*? No, of course you didn't. At the deepest level, you knew of their innate wholeness and the infinite potential they contain.

How we develop and the kind of person we develop into is a result of those seemingly trivial (and sometimes not-so-trivial) moments when our safety is perceptually or overtly threatened. Again, how we interpret those moments stems from a primary biological directive to belong; the resulting decisions we make about ourselves and the world in order to belong dictate the reality we live in. With this underlying dynamic being a part of our human operating system, how then do any of us grow beyond the limitations that our fear creates?

I'll tell you.

If you want to claim the life you were born to live, you're going to have to take a leap of faith and decide that you were born whole and complete. You also have to realize that at some point early on you decided you weren't that. You did this to make sense of significant or even excruciating pain from the rejection you felt. This decision happened in one moment. And it is this experience that is the origin of your inner opposition.

Why might it be important to identify the origin of this inner opposition? Because once your logical mind pinpoints the absolute onset of your inner opposition—the turning point when you went from being whole and complete to fearing that you were faulty, stupid, a burden, not good enough, incompetent, mediocre, or anything of the like—then you have greater access to choice. You can reason with yourself and remember that underneath all your fears and false beliefs, there is a whole-and-complete you that you can *choose*. At the very same time, it's equally important to know that the choice to not choose inner opposition is entirely possible without recognizing its origin. But it can help.

With this understanding, let's do a brief exploratory exercise together.

The Memory of Rejection: An Exercise

A Self-Care Message: Answer these questions *only* if recalling the past isn't severely triggering for you and proceed only as far as you feel comfortable.

- Take a slow, deep breath and let yourself unwind and relax.

- Go back to your absolute earliest and most vivid *feeling memory* of rejection. Think about what was happening and how it made you feel about yourself.

- What decision might you have made about yourself in the moment? In other words, what did you decide about "who you must be" in order to make sense of what was happening to you?

- Now, notice how you thought about yourself and what you felt about yourself before the event? How did you regard yourself before the event? And notice how you decided to regard yourself after the event.

What did you see? And can you see that your earliest experience of rejection is the birth of your inner opposition—the internal belief structure that separates you from *you*? And if you can't identify that moment right now, I have a big request of you. I ask that you imagine that at some point in your life's trajectory, you decided something crappy and untrue about yourself to make sense of rejection or a feeling of *not wanted*.

Underneath all of that is who and what you were born to be: whole and complete.

However, you don't need to choose that whole-and-complete you yet, which may not feel like a choice at this point anyway. That's OK! The next few chapters will help you to find your way back to the ability to choose what is irrevocably true and beautiful about who you are. For now, all you need to do is agree that you took on inner opposition at some point in the past and that the decision you made as a result of enduring this perceived rejection is the source of your inner opposition. Most of all, I want you to see that the war you've been waging within yourself all your life—below the surface of your skills, talents, and accomplishments—doesn't come from a place of truth. It comes from an innocent yet false decision your younger self made.

Let's not let the past run your life anymore. Let's find out the core decision you made and change it.

THE CHOICES CHECKLIST

Where we're at in the journey:

- ☐ **Choice #1**: Choose to feel it out, not figure it out
  - ☐ **Process/exercise**: Three Steps for Feeling It Out: A Process for Integrating Choice #1 (page 50)
- ☐ **Choice #2**: Choose to know that there is no way things—or you—should be
  - ☐ **Process/exercise**: Four Steps to Freedom: A Process for Integrating Choice #2 (page 82)
- ☐ **Choice #3**: Choose to know that it's always working out for you
  - ☐ **Process/exercise**: Painting Forward: A Process for Integrating Choice #3 (page 99)

Chapter 8

THE DECISION THAT
CHANGED YOUR LIFE

There is only one cause of unhappiness: the false beliefs you
have in your head, beliefs so widespread, so commonly held,
that it never occurs to you to question them.

—ANTHONY DE MELLO, *AWARENESS*

Any time the topic of self-worth, self-esteem, or confidence would come up when talking with my Grandma Pat, she'd remind me of an old photograph that sat on her dresser. Alongside her ornately painted pysanky eggs, arrowheads she found in the fields where my grandpa's cattle grazed, and an eclectic stack of books ranging from political history to metaphysics were a few family photographs showcasing the fun times my cousins and I spent there on their farm. In one particular photograph, I'm about six years old and sitting on a front porch step with my three cousins: Brandon (ten years old), Alethea (seven), and Morley (five). Amid their exuberance and giant smiles, there I am—hands politely nested in my lap, head and shoulders shrunken as if to hide, and a sheepish smile that to my grandma pleaded, "Am I worthy? Am I good enough?"

When Grandma Pat would reference this picture, she'd shake her head with a smile and say, "Lordy o' mighty child, you were always so afraid of not being good enough. I just don't know where you got that from!"

Neither did I.

It was perplexing to both her and me. I received nothing but unconditional love from my parents and had been encouraged and supported in everything I did. My grandma was never slow to point that out: "You have parents who love you to bits and pieces and have given you everything you could ever need. Where on earth did you get that you're not good enough? Just stop it already!"

If only I knew where it came from . . . or how to stop.

That question—"Am I good enough?"—wasn't a literal question I asked myself. I didn't have words to verbalize the feeling of not enoughness back then. For me, inner opposition started early, as I believe it does with almost all of us. And the combined subtle sensation of self-doubt, fear, and uncertainty was like an imaginary friend that never left my side. It was a nebulous presence that kept me from raising my hand to ask a question in class, playing along with other kids at the neighborhood park, or asking our server for more napkins at our family's favorite Italian restaurant. I don't remember too much of my childhood other than a pervasive feeling of apprehension, and the worst part was, I couldn't even put my finger on what I was apprehensive about.

What is this? Where did it come from?

I realize now that the origin of my inner opposition isn't so mysterious. At a specific point early on in my younger years, I *decided* that I wasn't good enough, that I was lacking some intrinsic quality that made me worthy of acceptance and approval. I was terrified of exposing myself enough and getting validation that my fear was true. Raise my hand to ask a question and risk being laughed at? Are you kidding? No way. Get up from the table, go over to our server, and ask for more napkins? Absolutely not! She'll probably scoff at me for bothering her. Attempt to befriend kids at the park? What? Their rejection would be the worst of all! Nope. Instead, I just stayed quiet, followed the rules like a good girl, and ensured that I only did things that would make adults happy and keep kids' ridicule at bay.

Now, this is how fear manifested for me, but fear can show up in lots of different ways for everyone else. You could probably identify the impact your inner opposition had on you as you were growing up. Maybe you learned that being the class clown and getting people to laugh was a way of being accepted, or that practicing the violin for four hours a day to keep Mom happy was a way to stay safe. Or you intentionally defied authority and refused to try—and no, it wasn't that you were lazy; it's that you had a deep inborn fear that if you did actually try and then failed, you'd really prove to yourself and the world that you were a failure and the worst would happen: rejection.

Maybe you feel this fear now. Maybe you hold yourself back from stating your opinion or disagreement in a meeting when the leadership team is present. Or maybe you constantly judge yourself harshly—always noticing how you do or don't measure up and exhausted by your never-ending comparisons. Or maybe you stop yourself short from really claiming a vision for yourself because you don't believe you have a right to one. Instead, you default to thinking: *Who am I to actually create this? Who am I to actually make a difference?*

All this fear and every reason you hold yourself back simply come from that decision you made about who you are as discussed in the previous chapter—the decision based in fear or shame that altered the landscape of your life. So let's get to the bottom of it. We're going to identify a fundamental decision you made to make sense of feeling rejected, isolated, or not worthy of belonging at some point in the past.

I'm going to ask you a question, and I want you to be entirely honest. Take all the time you need to find the answer your survival brain has for you. Meaning, read this question, get quiet, and answer with the pit-of-your-stomach response that feels like inner opposition speaking. Don't let the brilliant, logical part of your brain talk you out of it. Listen for the negatively oriented answer that pops up instinctively. (Note: this is one of the *only* times I will ask you to listen to the fearful voice rather than the compassionate voice in your head.)

Question: What are you most afraid others might *find out*, *decide*, or think about you?

Now, be honest! Is it that you'd be found out as not as smart as people assume you to be, not as capable, that you don't know what you're doing, you're a burden (like me!), you're broken, you're a failure, you're a loser, or you don't fit in? Or would they suddenly realize that you're not good enough?

If you answered with anything that sounds like one or a few of these questions, then get excited, because we are getting somewhere! If you felt an inner argument emerge that sounded something like, "Ugh, it would be that I'm [insert your gut reaction answer]. Hmm, but wait, I've accomplished [example] and [example], so nah, that's not it," then welcome to the split self (which we'll cover in chapter 10). Most of us are in touch with inner opposition's answer, only to be silenced by the loving and empowering part of us that wants to facilitate forward movement in our life. That empowering, wise, truthful voice that's trying to talk you out of it is absolutely wanted *and necessary*, but you'll have to briefly set aside its wisdom so you can clearly see what's happening underneath the mess of all those crazy thoughts. Consciously listening for this voice of fear is very brave. Hearing what it has to say—giving your inner opposition the airtime it's often begging for anyway—will allow you to *choose* to no longer let it run your life.

Really sit with this question if the answer is not immediately clear, ruminate and let the answer come. You'll find that it will come to you not only in the form of thoughts, but it will also arrive as the *feeling* you know this fear to be. In all my years of coaching individuals and leaders from all backgrounds and walks of life, there has never been one person whose inner opposition didn't have an answer. This is what I usually hear:

"I'm worried that other people will find out I'm a failure. Even though I've accomplished a lot that would prove otherwise, I'm waiting for the other shoe to drop."

"I'm afraid I'll be found out as not smart and incompetent. I always feel like I'm not really 'one of them' at work, like they all have more expertise and experience than I do."

"Straight up, it's not being good enough. I've had it for a long time, I've been worried about it all my life."

"Mediocrity! I'd rather be dead than seen as average."

"I'm afraid of being found out that I'm a fraud and that the depth people think I have isn't actually there."

"That I'm unlovable. It's not easy to hear myself say that, but it's true."

"Worthless. I'm terrified that people will think I've no potential."

"Deep down I fear I'm stupid and boring. I've had so much pressure to make use of my smarts all my life that I'm worried I don't even know who I am."

"I feel I'm genuinely lacking. My spouse thinks I'm crazy because we've both accomplished so much and are very successful. But as much as we accomplish, I can't get away from this feeling."

"I'm afraid they'll find out that I don't really know what I'm doing. I do everything I can to prove my smartness, but I don't push my opinions. I acquiesce when someone pushes back on me, and then I work super, super, super, super hard to prove them otherwise."

"I'm different. I have a much different background than everyone else. I don't want to risk sharing my story and then worry that I've given reason for anyone to judge, thus reject me. My logical brain says that probably won't happen, but I flat out *refuse* to open up."

"I never understood this 'imposter syndrome' thing, I don't think I have it because I know I can do my job. But I still feel—and have always felt—like an outsider, that I'm different than everyone else, and I don't really fit into the mold."

In the previous chapter, I explained the event that happened with my mom where I subconsciously adopted the belief that I'm a burden—which simultaneously was the decision that changed everything for me. So that very same belief is exactly what I don't want people to find out about me. It sounds like this: *I'm afraid of being a burden. And somewhere deep down, I believe that I'm not good enough to deserve attention or belonging.*

In all the work I've done with clients and in all the conversations I've had with family, friends, and even the most impressive and successful movers and shakers in the world, I've realized that each of us has an answer to this question that maps back to a primal need to belong and avoid being shunned by others. And *it's OK! You're OK!* The reality is, each of us humans has a biological imperative to belong. Matthew Lieberman, one of the foremost authorities in the study of social neuroscience and author of the book *Social: Why Our Brains Are Wired to Connect*, argues that our need to be socially connected with others is so strong that it's one of *the* primary drivers of behavior.[1] I believe that it is for this reason that each of us inescapably imprints a fear-based

---

1   Matthew Lieberman, *Social: Why Our Brains Are Wired to Connect* (New York: Crown, 2013).

false belief about ourselves, that we are lacking or faulty in some way, to make sense of one of the most threatening experiences we could ever experience as young children—*rejection*, that deeply rooted dread we began to discuss in chapter 6.

So taking a deep breath in, I invite you to look at this question again: What are you most afraid others might decide, think, or figure out about you?

Whatever answer you derived or are in the process of deriving—whether it's a brand-new insight or an answer that you blurted out as easily as you can say your name—we now have extremely valuable information, the most *important* information, to launch from: you just identified what *you* believe about yourself. It's not just that you don't want others to think this about you, you believe this about yourself. And this leads us right back to your inner opposition. *The contents of your inner opposition are all based on a false, lack-based belief you fear is true.*

What? I hear you saying.

You may be well aware that you believe the things you just answered with—that you're not smart, not competent, that you don't fit in, or the like. Or maybe this inquiry is a wake-up call that you're hearing for the first time. The reality is, whatever you answered is what *you* fear is true about yourself, otherwise, you wouldn't have answered it.

If that's hard to grasp, try this:

Conjure up something you don't at all believe about yourself, something that wouldn't trigger you whatsoever if someone thought it about you. For example, if someone said to me, "You're an unloving mother," I would meet that statement with curiosity and shock, but I wouldn't feel triggered or threatened because I don't believe that to be true at all. I *know* I'm a loving mother. Now, because I don't believe that I'm unloving, I'm not affected by how the outside world may perceive my love for my children. And I would never answer the question "What are you afraid other people would think about you?" with "unloving mother" because no part of me fears that it's true. However, if someone said, "You're not qualified enough to write this book"—if I didn't know what I now know—I would feel a punch to the gut sprinkled with a hint of shame. It would have been triggered because it electrifies my old deep-rooted limiting belief that says, *I'm not good enough.*

For me, this "not good enough" story is a belief structure I imprinted years ago. Check it out for yourself. What underlying beliefs are dragging you down? Whatever you honestly answer is our way through the back door to excavate the uncomfortable beliefs that are operational in your life even if you're good at distracting yourself from them. Remember, to claim the life you were born to live, you have to identify exactly who you *aren't* and what's *not* true—you have to pinpoint the fears and false beliefs of your inner opposition. And—as real as it all feels, it's all false.

But hold up, Amy, this stuff is true.

If that was your initial response, all good. I feel you. For years I was trapped in a web of wonky beliefs, too tangled to discern the threads of truth from fear. There was nothing any one of my beloved family members or friends could do, say, or provide that could genuinely convince me of my enough-ness, regardless of the quality or quantity of proof they provided. Why? Because my inner opposition had my sense of self on lockdown.

Inner opposition is wicked strong. Its sole job is to keep you safe from rejection—because remember, rejection feels like physical pain. Therefore, it does everything it can at every moment to keep you equally safe from environmental, physical, and emotional threats to social rejection. Inner opposition emerges as your well-meaning but horribly inaccurate soldier, tasked to keep you alive in the war of social threats, saving you not from strangers with sharp knives, but from colleagues with snide comments. Sadly though, your loyal soldier stays on guard and *busy*! Because it's constantly fighting a battle of its own creation.

Fortunately, us humans have evolved way past our caveman days and are capable of discerning the difference between hungry tigers and heartbreak. Humans have a capacity called conscious *choice*. We can consciously choose to *respond* to stimulus, not just *react* to it. We don't have to keep operating from the biological programming that says rejection is the same kind of threat as a tiger attack. But to exercise that capacity takes a bit of an understanding of our primal biological instincts, along with an ability to see our inner opposition for what it is: well-intended but completely inaccurate. So I'm going to ask you to temporarily suspend any and all conclusions about how your inner opposition defines you and keep an open mind so that together we can free you from the tangled web of beliefs you're caught in. You've had a lifetime of surviving your inner opposition, trying to disprove your false beliefs, while at the same time prove yourself worthy of belonging. That's a lot of practice in believing those fears as true. Sadly, practice doesn't make perfect in this case, it makes it feel *permanent*. Through years of surviving our inner opposition, we convince ourselves through practice and repetition those fears are true. And believing those fears and false beliefs to be true is exactly what keeps us from who we really are and the life we're meant to live.

THE CHOICES CHECKLIST

Where we're at in the journey:

- ☐ **Choice #1**: Choose to feel it out, not figure it out
  - ☐ **Process/exercise**: Three Steps for Feeling It Out: A Process for Integrating Choice #1 (page 50)
- ☐ **Choice #2**: Choose to know that there is no way things—or you—should be
  - ☐ **Process/exercise**: Four Steps to Freedom: A Process for Integrating Choice #2 (page 82)
- ☐ **Choice #3**: Choose to know that it's always working out for you
  - ☐ **Process/exercise**: Painting Forward: A Process for Integrating Choice #3 (page 99)

Chapter 9

UNDERNEATH THE HEADSET

True healing is not the fixing of the broken,
but the rediscovery of the unbroken.
—JEFF FOSTER, TWITTER, MARCH 2015

It's a guilty pleasure for my kids and me to watch the show *Try Not to Laugh*, a modern-day version of the popular 1990s TV show *America's Funniest Home Videos*. It features a compilation of funny blooper clips from YouTube or elsewhere—from kids saying ridiculously entertaining things to animals acting in unbelievable ways, all while a contestant is challenged to watch alongside the viewer without laughing or smiling. It's amazing the self-control some of these contestants exercise, able to remain deadpan in the face of the oddball antics while my kids and I are doubled over in laughter. Not all clips are laugh-out-loud worthy, but most of them are perfectly unpredictable, innocent, delightful, and sometimes shocking.

A kind of blooper that cracks us up every time is watching someone experience virtual reality (VR) through a VR headset, usually for the first time. There is something rather hilarious and mesmerizing about watching someone become completely immersed in a scene behind their digital lenses while simultaneously becoming oblivious to the actual world around them. To give you a good idea of this, imagine your own mom putting on a VR headset, comfortably sitting on her couch and resting her hands in her lap, when all of a sudden she sits up with a jolt, grabs on to the cushions for dear life, and screams as loudly and wildly as you've ever heard her. Despite your laughter and trying to console your mom over the sound of her own screams—"Mom! It's not real! You're OK!"—there is no amount of intervention, other than taking off the headset, that would get her to respond otherwise. In her private universe, there behind the virtual lenses, she was immediately transported from her living room to a world-class roller coaster of the most exhilarating kind. The only way for her to get off the ride would be to take off the headset.

It's comical watching someone at the mercy of a VR headset because we know they're ultimately safe and can choose to wear it or not. Because we trust our friends and ourselves enough to take the headset off if we've had enough of that reality, it's easy to be amused by their reaction. It's really all fun and games when it comes to virtual reality because the experience is pure perception. And because we know that what they are perceiving is not real, we don't take their reaction personally. Here's what I mean.

Imagine your friend comes over to try out your new VR headset. In this virtual reality, she begins by entering a beautiful, lush field of flowers enveloped by the sound of a peaceful breeze and occasional bird song when all of a sudden she's attacked by an angry swarm of bees. As your friend jolts from wonder to sheer terror, she begins screaming, swatting at the air, and then—*smack!*—she hits you in the face. Would you make a decision about your friend at that moment based on her reaction? Would you think, *What a terrible friend! Here she was, acting calmly and kindly, then out of nowhere she screams and starts swinging and slapping at me! She must be a resentful and angry person! She must have issues!*

No. You'd no doubt be inclined to laugh. You wouldn't take her reaction personally, and you wouldn't assume her character to be flawed based on this one experience. You would know that she was reacting to the scene in the VR headset. You'd understand that her actions and behaviors were a response to a perceived threat that her senses told her was real, and that it had nothing to do with you in the actual real world outside of the headset.

THE INNER OPPOSITION HEADSET

While all this VR stuff might seem amusing, the truth is that almost all of us have our own version of an inner opposition VR headset that we're unknowingly wearing—and it's programmed with thoughts and beliefs we discussed in chapter 6 that define inner opposition. For this reason, we're regularly reacting to its superimposed realities from a myriad of limiting negative beliefs. Beliefs such as:

- "I'm not good enough."
- "I'm not smart enough."
- "I'm less than."
- "I'm broken."
- "I'm incompetent."
- "I don't belong."

The moment you made *the decision that changed your life* (as you identified in the previous chapter)—when you took on a belief like one of these to make sense of an incident of perceived rejection—you took on the inner opposition you learned about in chapter 6. Taking on inner opposition really is akin to putting on an inner opposition VR headset. Why? Because inner opposition, the result of all the negative self-beliefs you adopted to ultimately stay safe and avoid rejection, is a made-up construct of the mind. And those negative self-beliefs make visible a VR you then figure out how to navigate. All beliefs, both negative and positive, act like lenses that influence your perception by adding meaning to your experience, making certain things in your perceptual vista pop while others remain hidden.

For example, if I look out the window right now and believe it to be a lovely day, my belief has my eyes tuned to the things that validate it as a lovely day—not a cloud in the sky, kids riding bikes down the street, birds flitting from branch to branch. Never mind the fact that the positioning of the sun leaves no shade to rest in. Never mind the fact that there isn't a calm breeze to enjoy. Forget that there is loud noise coming from the house under construction two doors down. If I believed it was a crappy day those negative aspects are the things I would have no doubt narrowed in on. Just like those VR headsets, beliefs serve as lenses influencing what you perceive and pay attention to. If you're old enough to recall the bright red View Master Classic Reel Viewer, it's much like that. We'd put the cherry red binoculars up to our eyes, insert one of the circular film reels, and voila! 3D nature landscapes or scenes from Disney movies layer upon our real life, convincing our child minds that Tinkerbell is, in fact, resting in our hand. When it comes to our inner opposition lenses, though, we're usually observing scenes that don't particularly serve us, often not realizing that they're no more real than VR.

This is what I really want for you to understand: when inner opposition is a part of your internal operating system, you're unknowingly wearing perceptual lenses that influence what you see, what you interpret, and how you navigate most aspects of your life. For example, with the very common inner opposition lens of "I'm not good enough," you might not be experiencing the threat of angry bees like your friend did with your VR headset, but instead, you experience situations where you:

- Prevent yourself from asking for help on a project for fear of appearing incompetent to your manager

- Refuse to speak up in a meeting among leadership so as not to sound stupid to your teammates

- Keep yourself from asking the person you like on a date because you're convinced she's out of your league

- Dwell on the fact that your colleague got promoted instead of you and fail to focus on the sizable bonus you received for completing a high-stakes project on time and within budget

- Stop yourself from stating your opinion at work because you imagine that your teammates' contributions are more valuable than yours

- Feel tremendous anxiety in delivering presentations because you're afraid of forgetting what you want to say and appearing to not know what you're talking about

- Avoid looking at yourself in the mirror because you always see what's wrong instead of seeing how healthy you actually are

Inner opposition lenses have you perceiving realities that could potentially expose you as not good enough *so you can avoid them* to ensure a sense of safety, approval, and belonging among others. In other words, what stands out as evident, or what becomes visible, is due to the inner opposition lenses through which you're seeing the world. You perceive and interpret who you are, as well as your surrounding reality, based on the inner opposition lenses you put on as a result of the decisions and beliefs you've made to stay safe and accepted by others. As you may also recall from chapter 6, every human's biological directive is to feel safe and accepted because rejection is literally painful. And so you unwittingly put on these lenses to avoid that pain. After wearing the lenses for so long, it's easy to assume those virtual realities as real, causing you to eventually believe that you're inherently faulty in some way. As compelling and convincing as those perceived realities appear to be, the truth is that underneath the superimposed perception from your inner opposition headset is an unbroken, unflawed, whole, and complete individual. In the same way your friend wasn't inherently faulty for reacting to angry virtual bees, you are not inherently faulty for perceiving yourself as *not-enough* in your own life.

Put another way, there was a point in time *before* you made the decision that changed your life, when you were existing as a whole and complete being, with no sense of faultiness, wrongness, or not-enough-ness. Have you witnessed an uninhibited, self-expressed child play and delight in life without any concern about what people think of them? For instance, have you ever watched the joy and playfulness that a young child embodies while they dance wildly to live music, or when they belt out songs they make up on the spot? That joy and freedom emerges from their unconditional self-acceptance, which is the result of unintentionally living as the whole and complete person they are. Each of us begins life in this untethered state, as a beautifully intact and full-of-potential canvas. That whole and complete *you*—the one who danced as if no one were watching, who made the decision that changed your life—is still there. Take off the inner opposition headset and what you will find is that whole and complete, worthy and deserving, resourceful and resilient human being who was already there before any decision you inadvertently made to be otherwise. In the same way your mom wasn't a coocoo bird for screaming wildly on her couch because she was on a virtual roller coaster, *you* are not broken, faulty, or inadequate for finding yourself in situations in which you see yourself to be inferior (and wanting to run from them like a bat out of hell).

But I get it. If you're unknowingly wearing inner opposition lenses, it's easy to mistake these realities for who you are. Most of us survive this inner opposition reality for so long we lose touch with the truth of our being—that we're whole, complete, worthy, deserving, resourceful, resilient, and *enough*. We forget that underneath our reactions to our false perceptions is a human being rooted in pure loving consciousness who loves and wants to be loved, who profoundly wants to feel at home in this world. After the thousands of conversations I've had with clients, family, and friends, I see clearly the predicament humans fall into while trying to ensure acceptance, belonging, and approval: we take on false limiting beliefs to keep ourselves safe from rejection, but we end up struggling to survive the superimposed reality caused by those beliefs. All the while, underneath the inner opposition brought to life by those same beliefs, we are each inherently *complete*. Many of us have just forgotten how to *know* that.

Choice #4: Choose to Know That You Are Already Complete

There is nothing to change, grow, or fix about who you are at the core. Your wholeness is already there. This is the fourth deliberate choice that will dramatically alter your life for the better: *choose to know that you are already complete.*

If you're going to take the leap to realize fulfillment and joy, you have to decide, right now, that underneath the headset of fear and false belief exists a perfectly whole and complete being, one who was capable of acquiring false beliefs to stay safe, and one who's capable of choosing otherwise. You don't have to know *how* to choose your whole and complete self just yet; we'll get to that in chapter 12. All I'm asking right now is that you acknowledge that an unbroken, worthy and deserving, resourceful and resilient, *enough* human being is there underneath the false perceptions you previously believed to be real.

What Does Whole and Complete Really Mean?

Whole and complete as an essence of being does not mean "perfection" by some archetypal standard. As we discussed in chapter 4, there is no objective way life, or *you*, should be—making mistakes, human error, and misperception are all a part of the human experience. Knowing that there is no objective way things should be keeps diagnoses like autism, birth defects, and mental illness from being "wrong." How could we say what is ultimately right or wrong, or true or not true, about existence—especially given that we can't even agree on the origin *of* or reason *for* consciousness! Appealing to logic here, all humans have more or less the same brain structure and sensory capacity, causing us all to appear to be on the same page about what *conscious* experience is. But we can't measure it or locate the origins of it; we really can't know anything about it other than our direct experience of it.

When it comes to conscious experience, all I can truly know is my own—and therefore assert that *I exist*. Do I know for certain that you exist? No, I don't. Instead, we're in agreement that you exist, and I like that agreement, but I can't get into your mind and have *your* direct conscious experience. I, therefore, cannot truly know anything about the nature of existence beyond my own direct experience.

Philosophical solipsism aside, we're each subjected to innocent ignorance about anything having to do with *being*-ness. We are limited by the bounds of human perception, which prevents us from determining the absolute truth about reality. We filter our life experience through lenses shaped by many—from grandparents to teachers to physicists and philosophers of many different persuasions. The varying hypotheses we are heir to span from explanations like the existence of Heaven and Hell to *Matrix*-style simulations to the existence of a multiverse. Exploring our true nature requires an appreciation of the mystery of consciousness and a humility that admits that "we just don't know what's true."

This is where *choice* comes into the picture.

If we can't know for sure the nature of our existence, why not *choose* an idea that allows for growth, possibility, and freedom? Why not choose to accept that we are, at the core, complete? Not *perfect*, but unbroken and capable beings wanting to love and be loved by others, capable of both mistakes and greatness.

How might this intentional choice make a real difference?

Motivated Perception Theory: The Research Is In

Because of what "motivated perception" research tells us, thanks to a study done by Yuan Chang Leong and fellow researchers Brent L. Hughes, Yiyu Wang, and Jamil Zaki, we have evidence that subjective experience is altered by motivation and we experience the world as we want or *choose* to see it.* The world I want to experience is one filled with love, compassion, peace, and joy. Creating this experience begins with what I decide to be true about who we truly are. This decision, then, is a doorway to a field of pure potential in which we locate our unbroken, whole, and complete selves. This is our playground for creating, transforming, growing, and thriving.

*Yuan Chang Leong, Brent L. Hughes, Yiyu Wang, and Jamil Zaki, "Neurocomputational Mechanisms Underlying Motivated Seeing," *Nature Human Behavior* 3 (2019): 962–973.

TURNING AWAY FROM TRUTH

"I remember being a happy kid when I was really young," my client told me as she looked down at the floor. "And then, I remember feeling very different, very less than, in second grade. I remember all of a sudden being so terrified of speaking up and being laughed at that I was constantly anxious around other kids. As early as seven, I taught myself to stay quiet and never rock the boat. And this is still who I am now at forty-five—I'm known for being the 'amiable leader.' I guess I didn't think I was good enough then, and I can see that I'm still choosing to believe that on some level now. The problem is, I have *no* idea how to choose otherwise."

This is my client's inner opposition in action. Before we deconstruct her statement to see what's going on, let's acknowledge that there was a period in time *before* the less-than state settled into her psyche. Whether the unworthiness took up residence in preschool or kindergarten or at another pivotal moment, the truth is that there was a point in time *before* she decided she wasn't good enough. That time was before she developed inner opposition and put on the headset of false beliefs to stay safe. It was the time in which she embodied a faultless, worthy, and deserving state of being.

1. **"I remember feeling . . . less than as early as second grade."** To feel *less than* implies there is a being underneath the overlaid feeling state of inadequacy. So there must be a *being* upon which to exercise a chosen feeling state.

2. **"I can see that I'm still choosing to believe that I'm not good enough on some level now."** *Still choosing to believe* implies that she knows she's in the driver's seat and that she has the option in perceiving a value-laden judgment about herself—or not.

3. **"I have *no* idea how to choose otherwise."** Choice is everything here, implying the existence of something else other than that which is being perceived. This statement suggests that she understands that a different choice would lead to freedom.

The *being* underneath our value-laden perception is the whole and complete canvas that each of us is at our core. Most of us instinctively feel the truth that there is more to who we are. We often feel there is something deeper—an essence that isn't fully embodied. We sense that there is a way of life that's easier than what is being lived, but the path to that truth, freedom, and vitality feels elusive. (These inklings are probably why you're reading this book!) But the only reason that path feels elusive is because your inner opposition headset is still on. Each of us has the ability to take it off, but it's impossible to exercise this ability unless we know about our whole and complete being underneath the superimposed reality. To break free, we must wake up to the fact that our suffering or struggle results from false perceptions—false perceptions resulting from the decision we made about ourselves to make sense of perceived rejection.

The moment you made that decision is what I consider to be the moment you turned away from truth. Turning away from truth can elicit different meanings for people. It might sound like a form of denial or resignation about reality. It could also appear to be an intentional act to numb, control, or sedate ourselves from unpleasant emotions or our complex inner world. In the living-on-purpose context, turning away from truth captures the natural consequence of believing the worst about ourselves. As I've worked through this process with countless clients, I can't help but refer to that moment in our life when we adopted inner opposition—the moment we formed a negative and untrue perception about who we are and disidentified from being utterly complete—as the moment we turned away from truth.

But don't despair. You're meant to wake up and return to the truth, which feels like home. This is a part of our shared human experience: to lose ourselves in the process of navigating life and have the exhilarating opportunity to rediscover and reclaim the truth of who we *really* are. Inherent in the hero's journey that each of us embarked upon at birth, we are meant to come home again—to find our way back to the shore of our whole and true self. Inner opposition is the necessary experience that introduces you to who you aren't so you can claim who you really are. (Because you can't know who you really are if you don't know who you aren't!) As you discovered in chapter 5, your thriving is predicated on duality. We require contrast to grow. Without the experience of inner opposition, you wouldn't have a reason to take your life by the horns and *choose to live on purpose*.

Would our life experience be truly meaningful if we floated along without the opportunity to learn and grow from mistakes and setbacks? No, that wouldn't be purposeful or productive at all. For example, one of my clients was a manager for a research lab at a university. As an extremely ambitious and motivated young woman, she was passionate about her career and wanted to be known as a leader who stood for operational excellence and efficiency. After returning from maternity leave, she was blindsided by a report from HR detailing a collection of negative feedback about her from many of her colleagues and cross-functional partners. Not only was she put on a performance improvement plan, but her scope of responsibility was also reduced, and she was stripped of her managerial responsibilities. She felt betrayed, confused, and angry. *How long have they been feeling this way?* she wondered. *And why did they wait until now to ambush me? After all, don't they realize how dedicated I am to the lab's success?*

Then, in what for her was a radical act to find meaning and purpose, she decided that instead of finding blame and harboring resentment, she would use this painful experience as a reason to do some honest, inward examination. Together we dove in deep to reveal her inner opposition and how it had been unintentionally driving unhelpful behaviors. With a big shift in perception, she discovered how her intentions and impact were incongruent and worked hard to align them so as to be the caring, courageous, and wise leader she intended to be. This growth gave her the clarity and confidence to make a big leap away from academia, and she is now on the fast track to executive management in one of the biggest companies in biotech. She admits that if it weren't for that painful wakeup call, and what felt like a devastating professional setback at the time, she wouldn't have had the reason to discover her blind spots and embody the awakened, compassionate soul that lived beneath her unacknowledged fear. She wouldn't be thriving in the way she is now.

In the same way that setbacks tee us up for growth, inner opposition is the manure that provides the fertilizer for our blossoming. So don't think of turning away from truth as a bad thing. And don't think that taking on false, limiting beliefs was a mistake that you could have avoided. As a child, with your young brain's limited ability to make sense of the complexity of life and relationships, coupled with your innocent perception, there was no way you could have. All parts of you were innocently trying to keep you safe.

And for all you parents out there: *you can't prevent your kids from interpreting the "what and how" of their own life experience, so don't be hard on yourself for the development of their own inner opposition.* I want to repeat this tender truth: each of us is doing the very best we can at every moment. If we could have done better, we would have! And if we would have known better, we would have done better. All of it is enough and always on purpose. So I invite you to drop any resistance you may have to how things have played out for you and consider inner opposition as a part of your soul's unfoldment and evolution.

Accepting this reality comes naturally when you embrace Choice #2, where you choose to know that there is no way things—or you—should be. Accepting this reality allows you to powerfully claim your true essence of being—a whole and complete individual beneath the inner opposition. Given that we're here in this conversation together, your job is to decide that how it has all come to be has been beautifully on purpose, and you're here now to get in touch with the already-complete you who is alive and well despite the false perception you've been surviving. The most direct path back to the truth is to recognize what isn't true so you can claim what is.

GET IN TOUCH WITH THE TRUTH: REFLECTIONS FOR INTEGRATING CHOICE #4

Looking back on our lives up until now is great for our own personal research and development and self-understanding—as opposed to being self-critical or conjuring painful feelings. When I look back at my own life, I see three distinct phases:

Phase 1: This was a short period in life, before about three years old, *before* I decided I was a burden and ultimately not good enough. This was the innocent phase in which I felt unconditional love for myself. Not because I practiced it actively, but because I didn't (and developmentally couldn't) perceive myself as broken, faulty, or inadequate. This is the phase when I was unconsciously living my truth as a whole and complete being, and therefore life was delightful and sweet.

Phase 2: After my first profound experience of perceived rejection around three years old, described in chapter 7, I made a decision about myself that I was a burden and not good enough. This is when I turned away from truth and adopted inner opposition to keep me safe from future situations where I might be rejected again. For the next twenty-five years, I would live my life as viewed through my own inner opposition glasses to attempt to stay safe.

Phase 3: After I took myself through the process to identify my false limiting beliefs and do something about it was when Phase 3 began. When I decided that I was already complete and consequently committed to freeing myself from an inner opposition VR headset, I claimed the life I was born to live. I stepped into a life of freedom, joy, and possibility.

I'm inviting you to prepare yourself for Phase 3 right here, right now. It doesn't take much more than:

1. Realizing you took on inner opposition at some point to stay safe and accepted, and

2. Deciding that underneath those inner opposition lenses, you always were—and always will be—whole and complete.

So with that, my question to you is: Who is the *you* underneath the fears and false beliefs you've acquired to survive perceived rejection? The *you* who is rooted in pure loving consciousness? What is the essence of you, that makes you *you*, beautifully unique from me and everyone else around you, yet stemming from the same loving consciousness from which we all arise? Who is the whole and complete individual within you who has been there from the moment you were born and will remain until the day you die? Who is the whole and complete individual who is there for you to claim? There is no story, act, or feigned personality to find; it's an essence of being that *feels* meaningful, purposeful, and *you*. And remember, because there is no way things, or *you*, should be—there is no "right" answer to find here! Think of it this way: if you're inspired to a thought or idea of what the true essence of you is, then inspiration is pointing you to the truth already. Why else would you want it? The right answer is the answer you *want* it to be, the answer that feels good at the thought of it being you.

For me, I've decided that my whole and complete essence has these four energies at the center: empowerment, wisdom, joy, and clarity. These are qualities of my whole and complete self that I have decided are unconditionally who I am because it *feels* right and true. What essence qualities will you choose to claim because it feels right? Feel this one out, don't figure it out.

If there are no specific qualities or words coming to you now to map to what feels right, that's A-OK. All you need to do is to be open to the existence of the state of being that is of unconditional enough-ness— the state of being that was the *you*—before you turned away from truth. There is no right or wrong way to do this. It just takes a curiosity and willingness to touch into the part of you before you made the decision that changed your life.

If you can't remember what it felt like before your world was rife with inner opposition, that's totally fine too. Then simply acknowledge a wholeness that was you when you came into being, a wholeness you unknowingly lived before you could acknowledge it, a wholeness that is there underneath practiced false perception. For now, feel it if you can, or simply acknowledge that it's still there. In chapter 11, I'll teach you how to claim it.

If you're having a hard time accepting the truth underneath your inner opposition headset and want to defend your perceived lack, then I lovingly ask you, would you rather prove your point of view or find peace? Would you rather argue for your limitations or claim a life of joy, freedom, and possibility?

Take the leap: choose peace and possibility. And join me in the next chapter where, through a client story, you'll see how that choice becomes possible.

STANDING ON THE SHOULDERS OF GIANTS

To suggest that beneath inner opposition and all its effects each of us is inherently whole and complete is an invitation that doesn't come without its research. "Who are we, *really?*" is a question that lives at the heart of most fields of study—from biology, psychology, and anthropology to philosophy and spirituality. The debate between the experts and sages dates back for centuries. Plato and Descartes believed that all humans were born with certain traits that occur naturally regardless of environmental influences. John Locke, one of the most influential philosophers of the Enlightenment era of the seventeenth and eighteenth centuries, believed that humans were born as blank slates and that we learn all our behaviors, both good and bad. Then in the 1870s, the founder of criminology, Cesare Lombroso, suggested that criminals were born "bad" and could be identified through the shape of their facial features. By the time John Watson and B. F. Skinner helped establish the theory of behaviorism in the nineteenth century, the sentiment had swung sharply back to the idea that who we become is strictly due to conditioning and outside influences.[1]

This back-and-forth examination is classically known as the nature versus nurture debate, and due to recent research, the sharp distinction between the two is becoming blurred. For well over a century now, scientists have been interested in the causal relationship between behavior and biology, and only recently in the twenty-first century are they starting to get a handle on how experience influences gene expression. Studies in the field of epigenetics suggest that it's *both* nature and nurture that symbiotically determine our development. Epigenesists argue

---

1   J. B. Watson, "Psychology as the Behaviorist Views It," *Psychological Review* 20, no. 2 (1913): 158–177; B. F. Skinner, *Science and Human Behavior* (New York: The Free Press, 1953); Marvin E. Wolfgang, "Pioneers in Criminology: Cesare Lombroso (1835–1909)," *Journal of Criminal Law, Criminology, and Police Science* 52, no. 4 (1961): 361–391.

against the traditional idea that a person's genetics remain unchanged throughout their life, and instead hold that we are all born with a developing genome, one that adapts in response to its environmental context. Throw in research on attachment theory, a theory of early social development established by John Bowlby and Mary Ainsworth in 1958, and there is now empirical support for the fact that our earliest attachment relationships do, in fact, influence our development and personality.[2] *However, that influence does not set a developmental trajectory in stone.* According to clinical professors Dr. Dan Siegel and Dr. Alan Sroufe, "The brain continues to remodel itself in response to experience throughout our lives, and our emerging understanding of neuroplasticity is showing us how relationships can stimulate neuronal activation and even remove the synaptic legacy of early social experience... every starting point, however early one looks, is also an outcome; every outcome is also a starting point."[3]

This is all to say that while anyone can argue that we come into life with a set of genetic blueprints that can end up being activated by environmental context or not, nothing appears to be permanent about our beingness. Nothing says that there's a possibility that we enter into life inherently broken according to some objective standard, or that genetics, relationships, or experiences seal our fate in any particular direction. So if there is nothing inherent or permanent about who we are, then we can *choose* to see ourselves as a field of possibility—a field of possibility that in its essence is already whole and complete.

Remember, your choice is your truth—not the objective truth, but *your* truth.

---

2   Bethany Saltman, *Strange Situation* (New York: Ballantine Books, 2020), p. 77; Phillip R. Shaver and Mario Mikulincer, "Attachment Theory and Research: Resurrection of the Psychodynamic Approach to Personality," *Journal of Research in Personality* 39, no. 1 (2005): 22–45.

3   Dan Siegel and Alan Sroufe, "The Verdict Is In: The Case for Attachment Theory," *Psychotherapy Networker*, March/April 2011, https://www.psychotherapynetworker.org/magazine/article/978/the-verdict-is-in.

THE CHOICES CHECKLIST

Where we're at in the journey:

- ☐ **Choice #1**: Choose to feel it out, not figure it out
  - ☐ **Process/exercise**: Three Steps for Feeling It Out: A Process for Integrating Choice #1 (page 50)

- ☐ **Choice #2**: Choose to know that there is no way things—or you—should be
  - ☐ **Process/exercise**: Four Steps to Freedom: A Process for Integrating Choice #2 (page 82)

- ☐ **Choice #3**: Choose to know that it's always working out for you
  - ☐ **Process/exercise**: Painting Forward: A Process for Integrating Choice #3 (page 99)

- ☐ **Choice #4**: Choose to know that you are already complete
  - ☐ **Process/exercise**: Get in Touch with the Truth: Reflections for Integrating Choice #4 (page 156)

Part III

MAKING THE
ULTIMATE CHOICE

Chapter 10

THE TANGLED WEB WE WEAVE

Life is a lot like math. It's a simple idea,
but it can get complicated.

Meet Samantha: an incredibly smart, delightfully extroverted forty-something executive member of a successful tech company. She's quick as a whip, holds a visionary perspective of the industry, and commands the kind of attention and respect that military leaders earn. Her ability to articulate the abstract, inspire people with a grand vision, and captivate an audience with her storytelling make her the kind of thought leader young professionals aspire to be.

Folks who know Samantha assume she has it *made*. Her unapologetic self-expression, refreshing authenticity, and wild professional success is clear evidence that this woman thrives. Her big bets turn to big wins (mostly), she has a loyal and loving tribe at work and at home, and she makes a ton of money.

A few years ago, Samantha reached out to me with the expressed goal of wanting to improve her "executive presence." Having gotten to know Samantha and understand the power of her influence in the industry, I was rather intrigued with her ask. Emerging leaders were clamoring to have her mentor them on this very topic—she was viewed as the innovator who had practically written the book on it. I sensed that the term "executive presence" was rich with meaning for her, and I was keen to find out what that was.

"*Executive presence* feels like a guise for something more important. Double-click on this for me. What are you *really* after?" I asked.

Samantha answered without skipping a beat.

"My mind works ridiculously fast. For every given topic, I see a vast web of connections and the words just stream with the power of a fire hose—big picture, tangents, all of it. The problem is, I can't modulate what I say. My internal 'overseer' has no ability to filter. It's *very* challenging for me to moderate what I say. I have an inner gauge, but it's always too late. Our PR team gets freaked out when I'm invited to speak at a conference or sit on a panel because as much as I have people hanging on my every word, they don't want me to leave with my foot in my mouth. I need more focus, more discipline, and measured articulation."

I immediately thought of the quote by Viktor Frankl, the Austrian neurologist, psychiatrist, and Holocaust survivor: "Between stimulus and response there is space. In that space is the power to choose our response. In our response lies our growth and our freedom." It sounded like Samantha needed to harness and grow that "space between" impulse and action and find within herself a new perceptual muscle to *choose* her response. To Samantha, executive presence represented a calm and grounded awareness of the totality of her expertise and the ability to deliberately choose to deliver her message with power and grace.

"Talk to me about your experience when you're on stage or on a panel. What is it like to have so much mental momentum but little control of the flow?"

Samantha's shoulders softened and her face eased into a subtle expression of gratitude and relief. I got the feeling right then and there that she had felt completely alone in her mental whirlwind, surviving an inner reality that she feared very few might understand.

"It's gotten worse as I've gotten older and more successful, which seems counterintuitive given that I'm an expert in my field and I'm wicked smart. When I'm asked an exciting question during an interview, say, I have this frenzy of information bubble up in me, and I go into this overdrive mode. My head feels super busy, and I have no real oversight. Luckily, the words are generally dazzling, but I can't censor the output. It's only after the interview that I reflect, 'Gah! I shouldn't have shared that!' It's been manageable so far, but I'm afraid the wheels are going to come off. What *could* happen kinda freaks me out. It feels like I'm holding back a tidal wave."

I took it all in and marveled at what I was witnessing. Here she was, a successful female executive in Silicon Valley with the perfect life and professional trajectory, and she was silently struggling.

"Let us be kind, one to another, for most of us are fighting a hard battle."

These wise words by nineteenth-century British author Ian Maclaren, commonly misattributed to the philosopher Plato, poignantly capture a deep truth about humanity.[1] Beneath the convincing exterior of every person on the planet lives a rich world that is largely inaccessible to others, a complex internal reality rife with aspirations, fears, memories, histories, tragedies, regrets, meaning, reflections, and unanswerable questions. People are quick to assume that if the cover looks good, then the book will be good too. As book covers can't fully communicate the essence, complexity, and meaning woven together within the pages, our covers—our outer images—can't fully communicate the rich inner complexity that has us reaching for success or running from

---

1   Ian Maclaren, quoted in *News and Courier* (Charleston, SC), p. 4, November 27, 1947.

pain. It was clear that Samantha was seeking freedom from an internal reality she couldn't wrap her mind around.

Now, if I wanted to strictly coach her to practice new behaviors, I'd suggest a game plan that included a lot of meditation to strengthen her overseer while expanding the internal space between stimulus and response. By doing so, we would help her access the choice to *respond*, not react, to all the information in her head. A strict executive presence coaching approach would also include concerted exercises in dialogue that required her to pause and think long and hard before she spoke in a measured and controlled way. With enough practice we could most likely train her psyche to fall in love with "the pause" and use that space to mentally articulate a response before saying it out loud.

But I didn't want to simply fiddle with effects and ameliorate symptoms, and my gut was that she didn't either. I knew very well that the root of her challenge went deeper than her mental and verbal habits. Sure, we could take a band-aid approach and tweak the effects using meditation and lots of drills and reflection, but I knew improved verbal behaviors would not get her to the freedom and control she longed for. There was something bigger going on and it had to do with the relationship she had with herself. I had to find out more.

"Tell me what 'fight or flight' means to you. What is that experience in your world?"

Her eyes got as big as silver dollars, as if I were a fortune teller revealing a hidden secret about her life that there was no way I could know unless I was "legit."

"I'm shocked you picked up on that. *It's all the time.* I have this crazy unresolved fear of not being understood that constantly triggers a super strong fight or flight response. But this makes absolutely no sense! I'm typically quick on my feet when I'm communicating with people."

"It seems paradoxical for sure—to know you're super smart and good with words while at the same time constantly fearful that you're not being understood. When have you felt this kind of dissonance in the past?"

Samantha then proceeded to share a piece of her story.

Samantha's aunt, her mother's older sister, died in a drunk driving accident when Samantha was eleven months old. Samantha's mom and her sister had been very close, especially as adults, because they were both single mothers whose husbands had left the picture early on. When her aunt was killed, Samantha's mother felt a strong responsibility to adopt her fifteen-year-old nephew. At eleven months old, Samantha became a sister to the boy who was once her cousin. With no father figure present in Samantha's life, her older cousin ended up having a tremendous influence on her. Today in her mid-forties, Samantha has no conscious recollection of the tragic loss of her aunt and how it came to be that she instantly had a brother. All she remembers of her very young years is how she *felt*: uncertain and one step behind the curve.

"My cousin was a piece of work. I can only imagine why—he had lost his mom to a senseless and avoidable car accident and no doubt struggled with anger and resentment. But I think he projected his pain and anger onto me. He didn't give me any room to have knowledge or be an expert in something; he was constantly wanting to one-up me. Probably to feel important. I mean, he was a teenager who now had to share his life with an annoying little kid and contend with the loss of his mom. It couldn't have been easy for him, and he surely didn't make it easy for me."

Samantha had countless memories of encounters with her cousin where he would deflate her sense of pride and excitement with biting comments about how stupid she was, repeatedly claiming that she didn't know anything and was always wrong.

As we discussed the feeling states of "uncertain" and "behind the curve" that overshadowed her younger years, I asked how those feelings parallel her present-day challenges with modulated speech.

"Those feelings are exactly what I'm trying my hardest to disassociate from in my day-to-day. Look, I've had years and years of therapy to heal from the pain of my childhood, and I don't think I need to make any more sense of my past, but I'm at a loss for connecting my upbringing to my executive presence problem and am unclear of where to go from here."

Samantha looked over at me with a tired willingness. Her eyes glimmered with a mix of hope and resignation, wanting both an answer and an approach that made sense. For me, the connection was as clear as day, as was the solution to her executive presence issue. *Her inner opposition had become all-consuming.* And though she had learned to survive it in a high-functioning way, she had little cognitive bandwidth for thoughtful and measured speech, especially when she was in a reactive state, triggered by the fear of not being understood. As a child, she learned that to feel accepted by her cousin and be acknowledged by her own mother, she had to be smart and quick. I had to help her make sense of all this: her past, her inner opposition (which she knew nothing about at this point), and how that tied in with her aspirations for being more focused, articulate, and structured. It was time to connect the dots in a comprehensive way.

"Samantha, I'm going to ask you a question and I want you to answer it from your fight or flight brain—no logical or rational part of you can talk yourself out of this answer, OK?"

She nodded in agreement.

"What are you afraid others will ultimately think or decide about you?"

Before I could finish the question, she blurted out, "That I'm stupid!"

I paused a long time. Several seconds. "Samantha . . . you do realize that's what you believe about yourself, right?"

She looked at me like I had two heads.

"Otherwise you wouldn't have said it," I continued. "If you genuinely knew your intelligence, you wouldn't be concerned how others perceive your intelligence; it wouldn't ever register on the radar. Think of it this way: You didn't say they would decide that you're *funny*, and you know why? Because you know you're funny. For that reason, there is no conflict about humor for you. If someone told you they thought otherwise, you'd think that's their issue and you'd shrug it off. You wouldn't think twice."

Her posture seemed to settle deeper into her seat, and she started to nod her head as if something was beginning to come into focus. I could see that she was ready to hear more.

"This unacknowledged negative belief lives within you, deep inside, even though it's not chosen by your conscious mind. You most likely solidified this belief when you were young, trying to make sense of feeling uncertain and behind the curve from the interaction dynamics between you and your cousin. Even though this has nothing to do with him in your current reality, the carry-over is you're still unconsciously fighting this belief that you're stupid, particularly when the stakes are high. I'll guarantee that this internal fight is the source of your mental whirlwind and firehose speech. You're unknowingly working hard to hide so-called stupidity with smartness and speed. You're desperate to keep this from being found out and the overwhelm of your fear mutes your functioning overseer when the pressure is on."

This all made complete sense to Samantha—except for one thing: "Why am I so afraid of being seen as stupid when my logical self knows that I'm not?"

Ah, the tangled web we weave. Samantha was giving voice to an exasperating paradox in which our inner opposition feels so real, but our logic tells us otherwise. Let's dig a little deeper to understand this paradox, a paradox you may be wrestling with too.

STRATEGIES THAT KEEP US SAFE

You might not be a fast-paced tech executive, and you might not have had to compete with your cousin for your mom's attention, but regardless of your current circumstances and past experiences, developing and surviving inner opposition is a reality all of us face. And there is absolutely no blame to impart here on anyone. As we have discussed earlier, each of us is hardwired to connect and seek belonging—and we're doing the best we can, inner opposition and all, in every moment. In our young years, we're navigating life with an undeveloped ability to make sense of all the complexity and nuance that make up our relationships and life situations, *while instinctively avoiding rejection like the plague.* Put those facts together and it's inevitable that we form an inner opposition as we try to make sense of our reality and avoid rejection. In the same way Samantha's cousin was struggling to find acceptance by putting Samantha down to make himself feel worthy of belonging, Samantha took on the belief that she was stupid and thus learned to compensate by thinking quickly and proving her smarts. Fast-forward to today, and unconsciously conditioned within her is an unacknowledged identification with being stupid, counterbalanced by a conscious belief that she's wicked smart. This is the maddening paradox. This is the nature of inner opposition.

Now, although anyone could say Samantha has ultimately created a successful life, the truth is she's been inadvertently trapped in a false paradigm and struggling with the unwanted effects of unknowingly believing she's stupid. Samantha's need to prove her smartness, coupled with not being able to modulate what she says when the stakes are high, have formed a way of being that isn't rooted in truth. What's true is that she is—and always has been—perfectly whole and complete. Every day of her life, she has been capable, competent, worthy, deserving, and enough. However, after so much time grappling with such a painful core belief about herself, she's just forgotten that. Instead, she continues to demonstrate her smartness with velocity and wit, strengthening her belief of being wicked smart. But as long as she's trying to *prove* being wicked smart, she's preserving her fear that underneath it all she's not that.

This is what happens when we're constantly trying to prove anything—the sheer act of proving something necessitates the existence of its opposite. Samantha's need to prove her smartness is ultimately an *act* to keep from being found out. But the act keeps the false belief alive. Acts like this, acts that we take on to stay safe from rejection, are defined as survival mechanisms, and though they may appear to temper the effects of a false belief, they fan the flames of its existence.

Survival mechanisms are as creative and varied as we human beings are, and they're continually adapting to help us best survive the superimposed realities of our inner opposition. To keep others from seeing and then believing the false, limiting things we decided about ourselves, we take on acts or ways of being to prevent others from catching on—with all of this being an elaborate effort to stay safe from rejection.

To break free of the tangled web—the false paradigm we construct for our safety and ultimately get trapped in—we need to get clear about the *lived* effects of inner opposition. We need to see with clear eyes the reality our inner opposition VR headset generates. To do this, we have to identify all the survival mechanisms we've developed as a way of hiding our core false belief. It's worth doing the work because this false belief and all the fear it's based on is the food that keeps our inner opposition alive and operational.

Try this: recall that decision you pinpointed in chapter 8, the one that changed your life. Samantha discovered hers when she backtracked and realized that she had unknowingly decided that she was stupid. Get in touch with that belief right now and ask yourself this question completely, honestly, and for all time:

How do I show up in the world? What do I do to keep others from thinking,
deciding, or finding out that I am _____
[insert decision here]?

Everything you answer with is a survival mechanism. Survival
mechanisms are things like:

- I don't share or offer up much. I keep quiet most of the time.
- I debate everything I'm told.
- I have to have the last word.
- I make a joke of everything.
- I put everyone's needs before my own.
- I apologize for everything and am self-deprecating.
- I do everything I can to be seen as exceptional.
- I do everything I can to not take up space or draw any attention to myself.
- I refuse to lose.
- I don't take risks, and I don't put myself out there.
- I worry about what everyone thinks, constantly.
- I never ask for help. I do everything on my own.
- I second-guess my decisions and answers.
- I triple-check my work.
- I overanalyze and end up with analysis paralysis.
- I don't show my emotions.
- I can't feel my emotions.
- I don't have preferences; I'm happy when everyone else is happy.
- I give and I give and I give.

- "Rest" is not a word in my vocabulary. I'm a hyper-achieving productivity machine.

- I'm on a never-ending quest for more status, more money, more knowledge, and more prestige.

When behaviors are inadvertently employed to keep you *safe* from any form of rejection, then they are acts rooted in fear. This makes them survival mechanisms. There is observable rejection, like being dumped by your girlfriend via a text message. And then there is the fear of rejection, which may never actually come to pass. To the social brain, the fear of rejection can show up as fearing negative judgment, humiliation, a tarnished image, negative comparisons, disdain, or disapproval—anything that doesn't deem you favorable or potentially worthy of *belonging* to a particular group, tribe, or network.

So back to the big question, the question that was key to helping Samantha understand the mystifying paradox between her inner and outer worlds:

What am I afraid others will ultimately think or decide about me?

Now let's ask it in a more comprehensive way:

Why am I still so afraid of being found out as faulty, not-enough, or inadequate when my logical brain understands that I'm already complete? How can both beliefs feel true at the same time?

For each of us, the short answer is that survival mechanisms murk up what we know to be true about who we are and what genuine success really is. Our real self continuously pings us with the signals of our innate wholeness and well-being, but there's interference with receiving its pure frequency. And with a lot of practice living with false perception and enough time surviving inner opposition, we mistake our survival mechanisms for actual strengths. One of the challenges with this is that when our so-called successes are fueled by fear-based behaviors designed to keep from being found out, it's hard to own and embrace them. It's hard to feel at peace with them.

Why?

Because those actions and their results didn't arise from an understanding of and identification with our wholeness. They arose from a fear that we're not whole—and may never be!

I can't tell you how many people admit to me that even though their life looks great on paper, they are haunted by a nagging feeling that they're either not good enough, it's not real, it was all luck, or it's not enough. And yet the proverbial carrot continues to dangle in front of them, like the achievement carrot. "If I can just get this promotion, I will finally feel settled and at peace!" Well, the promotion may happen, but when it does it inevitably presents a whole new slew of challenges, rife with opportunities to prove yourself evermore . . . and so here we go again. When survival mechanisms are running the ship, we tend to need more confirmation or proof that we're OK—so we work more, work harder, achieve more, make more money, and believe that the next big thing will finally lead us to stable ground. That's when we can finally sit back and enjoy the fruits of our labor.

But that's all a false premise.

For the first twenty-eight years of my life, as I described earlier, I struggled with my own inner opposition. Deep down I had a fear I wasn't good enough and developed the survival mechanisms of perfectionism and hyper-achievement. I came to believe that to be perfect, to do perfect, and to be highly successful would secure others' approval and ensure a sense of belonging. *If I can just succeed enough, then everyone's admiration will ensure my safety.* Now to be clear, I didn't consciously think this way on a day-to-day basis, uttering these words to myself.

But still, this unconscious survival-based reasoning was the driving force behind most of my thoughts, words, and actions.

So you can see how this can get a little messy. When we're unaware of our inner opposition, we unwittingly confuse our noble-looking survival mechanisms as core strengths arising from authentic essence. *I must be a really driven, hyper-achieving, success-oriented individual,* I thought. Never mind the toll it took on my health. Never mind my inability to take a break from studying or work projects to enjoy my weekends or holiday vacations with my family or husband. Forget that I struggled with a persistent anxiety, so sure that all my success would fall away or I would hit a dead end at some point in my professional future. *What happens when my luck runs out?* I couldn't trust the integrity of my achievements because a majority of my drive arose from the unconscious need to compensate for my belief that I wasn't good enough. My survival mechanisms might have had me succeeding by conventional standards, but in no way was I winning. I was exhausted to the bone because my so-called strengths were the product of survival mode. That's not thriving!

As we go through life and succeed in this way, we contend with an unidentifiable confusion. We can't clearly see what's guided by our wholeness (love and truth) and what's guided by our perceived sense of lack (fear). It's like we're operating in the dark. But here's the great news: the invisible can be made visible. Confusion can dissipate like mist on a sunny morning. The chasm we feel between our true self and our fearful self can be mended once and for all.

There are just a few more crucial things to understand first.

ENTER: THE SPLIT SELF

I often hear in coaching conversations that clients feel like they've got two people inside of them: one part believing that they are capable, good enough, or competent, and another part fearing that they're not any of those things. Someone once told me that their inner dialogue felt like a ping-pong match, going back and forth between confidence and fear. "Sometimes I have no idea what part of me is going to run the show when the pressure is on," one client reported. If you've ever felt like you've got a conflict raging inside of you, it's because of the *split self*. In my years of work with people, I have come to see that this split happens because we're attempting to weave together our sense of self based upon two paths of perception:

1. **Truth and possibility.** Whether we realize it or not, all of us have a direct line to the truth of our being. We are whole, capable, worthy, deserving, enough, and complete. And as we allow this truth to permeate our thinking and feeling, we begin to see life through a lens of openness and optimism that brings all manner of opportunities and possibilities into view.

and

2. **False, limiting beliefs.** These are the false beliefs that we're afraid are true, and that give rise to the survival mechanisms we develop to hide them from being discovered. Inner opposition—that internal resistance to our inherent worthiness—is one of our chief strategies for managing our false beliefs and the fear that accompanies them.

Dependent on your circumstances and what you're dealing with in a moment, you can be resolutely rooted in truth or staunchly stuck in fear. And both can be live at the same time. Your sense of self is fluid and dynamic and ever-changing, depending on what you choose to focus on. This is why it can feel like a mess!

THE DIFFERENCE BETWEEN TRUTH AND FEAR

Making sense of this dichotomy and freeing ourselves from the false paradigm created by fear and inner opposition requires the ability to discern what's rooted in truth from what is not. But let's be honest, it can be hard to catch what you're believing about yourself in a given moment. I mean, life is loud and busy! It would take a significant amount of attention to exercise the kind of meta-observation required to say, "Oh, goodness me, there I go again! I'm aligning with a false belief about myself—I'm believing I'm not good enough in this moment. Well shucks, isn't that silly?"

Now, c'mon! That kind of awareness isn't often available in the heat of life's attention-grabbing moments—like when you walk into a room full of strangers at a conference, kick off a meeting with stakeholders you haven't met yet, or sit down at a crowded dinner table at your friend's hosted salon to facilitate a conversation titled "Intellectual Discourse on the Ethical Dilemmas of Artificial Intelligence" (yep, I did that). You're busy living your life, and unless you're an extremely practiced mindfulness meditator, your mind may be moving too fast to catch crappy self-beliefs the moment they're engaged. As Daniel Kahneman wrote in his book *Thinking, Fast and Slow*, "The often-used phrase 'pay attention' is apt: you dispose of a limited budget of attention that you can allocate to activities, and if you try to go beyond your budget, you will fail."[2]

Not that catching crappy beliefs is beyond your attentional budget, or that you will fail if you try—not at all! I'd like you to consider that instead of devoting your attentional bandwidth to your thoughts, the next best thing is to tune into what you're feeling. Just like we learned in chapter 2, *feeling it out* is the path to your authentic self. In this case,

---

2   Daniel Kahneman, *Thinking, Fast and Slow* (New York: FSG, 2011).

feeling it out means looking downstream to the *effects* of aligning with your false self, when survival mechanisms are in play, to notice how they make you *feel*. I recommend this only because I find that it's easier to be more sensitive to how you're feeling than to what you're believing in a moment.

Put another way, in order to claim who you *authentically* are and step into a life of greater power, love, clarity, joy, and peace, you must be able to *feel* the difference between an action arising from truth (your essence) versus a survival mechanism based in fear. This kind of sensing and discernment requires you to recognize that your survival mechanisms are distortions of your essence and can lead you to make choices that are restrictive and fear-based.

Here's a breakdown of how it feels when you're in touch with your true essence, when you are embodying your wholeness and completeness rather than resisting it:

- Your perception—your impressions and sensing of what you're experiencing—isn't guided by lack or faultiness. Instead, you're open to the world around you.

- The thoughts, words, and actions that result from your perception are all *aligned*. You don't feel the internal friction or anxiety that can bubble up when you're thinking or saying one thing and doing another.

- Fear of failure is transformed into excitement for possibility and momentum.

- You feel spacious—mentally and emotionally.

- You feel clear.

- You feel powerful.

- You feel compassion for yourself and others.

- You can feel that you're rooted in truth and love because you feel *energized*! And in any given moment, you may find yourself tapped into a kind of energy that feels nothing short of infinite.

Conversely, when you're emotionally triggered, overly identified with your false self, and immersed in inner opposition, you're likely to deploy survival mechanisms to keep others (and yourself) from thinking you're inadequate in some way. As we all know, the energy required to hide is exhausting, and often puts a wedge between ourselves and others.

As I shared earlier, I've decided that my essence is of empowerment and joy, and I've discovered that my inner opposition stems from an old false belief that I'm not good enough. Here's how in-alignment and out-of-alignment dynamics can look for me.

When I'm living in my essence, the qualities that emerge in my experience with others are generosity, care, loving attention, and an energizing investment in others. When there is no part of me triggered into a need to prove that I'm enough, then these qualities arise from a place of unconditional love and truth; I am literally *being* joy and empowerment in those moments. When this happens, I draw from an infinite reservoir of energy, insight, and inspiration, and it feels energizing. I feel clear and powerful, yet very grounded and peaceful.

On the flip side, if I'm contending with the fear that I'm not good enough in a moment, that I need to prove my worthiness to this person or prove myself in this situation, then those empowering qualities—generosity, care, and loving concern—become distorted. Generosity appears as desperation, care turns to neediness, and loving attention morphs into people-pleasing. They cross over the line from love to falsehood. My survival mechanisms are warped versions of my essence qualities that are deployed to survive a false idea that I'm not enough.

The consequences of that distortion feel life-draining, not life-giving. On the outside, anyone witnessing both scenarios would effectively see the same behaviors and resulting conversations, but the *energy* from which the behaviors and conversations arise are of two different realities, one of thriving and one of surviving. And for many people, the difference is acutely felt.

Case in point: another example of distortion is the distinction between confidence and arrogance. Everyone wants to be confident; no one wants to be arrogant. Why? Because confident people are inspiring, capable, and trustworthy. Arrogant people are abrasive, obnoxious, and annoyingly self-interested. But what's interesting is if you do a rudimentary observation of both confident and arrogant individuals side by side, their behaviors and actions can look pretty similar at first glance: they both tend to speak up, they both tend to create momentum, and they both have an impact on others. But despite how they look, these two people sure do *feel* different to outside observers!

As with every state of being, the quality and experience of that state depends upon the relationship we have with ourselves. The writer Anais Nin is noted for saying "We don't see things as they are, we see them as we are."[3] Confidence is a state of being that arises from a knowing of our completeness, where we feel naturally capable of engaging with a given person, situation, or circumstance. When we're rooted in truth, we feel energized, calm, present, and infinitely resourced. *This is power.* And it leads to truly empowering conversations and positive impact that lasts.

The opposite is true of arrogance. When someone is arrogant, I often hear people say that it's just because the person is insecure. Yes, but it goes deeper. Now knowing how inner opposition works, think

---

3   Anaïs Nin and Wayne McEvilly, *Seduction of the Minotaur* (Denver: A. Swallow, 1961).

about the kinds of false beliefs that would foster insecurity and the tendency to don a mask of arrogance (as a survival mechanism) to hide that insecurity. Most likely, one would harbor deep-down beliefs that they're incompetent, inadequate, and unworthy. And because these fear-based beliefs and the actions that result from them aren't rooted in truth, they feel off-putting at best.

FREEDOM FROM ENTANGLEMENT

Samantha had been caught up in a tangled web of conflicting beliefs and perceptions for longer than she cared to recount, but she did break free. The tug-of-war between her younger self (who felt stupid) and her adult self (who knows she isn't stupid) had finally become too exhausting. And the dynamic of feeling *not-enough* and *enough* all at the same time had become so painful that she reached out for help. Her story tells a tale for all of us to take heart in.

Inner opposition is not a life sentence! Nor is the split self a life sentence. As you'll recall from our first look into inner opposition, both these strategies offer the necessary experience of living who you aren't so you can claim who you really are. You're here to claim the life you were born to live, not to be a helpless victim to false perception!

The key to claiming who you really are is being able to choose truth over fear. *Easier said than done*, you may be thinking. Fair enough. But in the next chapter, I am going to show you how this all works.

THE CHOICES CHECKLIST

Where we're at in the journey:

- ☐ **Choice #1**: Choose to feel it out, not figure it out
    - ☐ **Process/exercise**: Three Steps for Feeling It Out: A Process for Integrating Choice #1 (page 50)
- ☐ **Choice #2**: Choose to know that there is no way things—or you—should be
    - ☐ **Process/exercise**: Four Steps to Freedom: A Process for Integrating Choice #2 (page 82)
- ☐ **Choice #3**: Choose to know that it's always working out for you
    - ☐ **Process/exercise**: Painting Forward: A Process for Integrating Choice #3 (page 99)
- ☐ **Choice #4**: Choose to know that you are already complete
    - ☐ **Process/exercise**: Get in Touch with the Truth: Reflections for Integrating Choice #4 (page 156)

Chapter 11

TAKE THE LEAP

If we would only see that all limitations are self-imposed
and chosen out of fear, we would leap at once.

—ADYASHANTI

"Here you are, Mike," I said to my client during one of our coaching conversations. "You're clearly aware that, a while back, you strapped on a set of 'I'm not good enough glasses.' You see the *what*, *why*, and *how* of your inner opposition, and you are *done* with it all. You get that *you* put the glasses on, and that *you* are the only one who can take them off. But now, somehow, *you've just tied your hands!* You know you have the choice to free yourself from false perception, but you're now making it extremely hard, if not impossible, to take the glasses off!" My unrelenting and loving honesty dissolved the tension in his posture. Mike smiled a big smile and nodded his head. By accurately mirroring where he was in his journey of transformation, he knew that I got both his eagerness and frustration. Over the course of our coaching together, Mike and I finally tipped the scales of transformation in his favor. However, the wisdom of the old saying "Awareness is half the battle" prevailed in that moment. Awareness wasn't enough for him to access a new choice at that point. Yet.

Guiding someone out of their inner opposition and getting them to a place of *accessible* choice is a journey of sorts, one that requires more than a simple five-step instruction manual. It's a process of discovery that asks us to look at ourselves and our lives differently—to try on a new perception. This is why I'm such a big fan of metaphors and analogies. Sometimes the simplest examples can help us to see through the mist of habitual thought patterns to a clearer understanding and awareness. Seeing ourselves anew requires us to exercise perceptual muscles that we didn't know we had. Case in point: Do you remember learning how to whistle for the first time? Hearing someone else whistle may have seemed like a magic trick. But then came the moment someone showed you how to do it. "You just have to do it like this . . ." So you tried it—and you probably tried it again and again. You pursed your little lips together a particular way. You pushed the air past your teeth and through your lips. And one day it happened! You whistled! It all came together—the information, the instruction, the felt experience of it, the new ability. Just as you unlocked the whistling ability for life, you are unlocking the ability to break free from the tangled web of perceptual limitations that have held you back.

I'm like your whistling coach. I can guide you, but I can't make the sound for you. You're learning to find and use a perceptual muscle that can help you to shift your entire life *before* anything in the outer world needs to change. So let's look briefly at the primary threads of the tangled web and how they come together . . . and how we got so far astray from the truth of who we are.

THE ARC OF THE UNWINNABLE QUEST: CONNECTING THE DOTS

Beginning in Part II, we learned about how we construct a false paradigm to guarantee safety and a sense of belonging in the world. Let's zoom out now to see the big picture and how all the pieces come together.

- Humans are hardwired to connect and belong with one another, which is why **rejection** is literally painful for us. For the entire span of our lives, we look out for and avoid things such as negative judgment, disdain, disapproval, isolation, lack of admiration, humiliation, embarrassment, failure, or losing. This primal fear of rejection significantly influences our perception and largely determines how we protect ourselves as we navigate the world.

- To make sense of an experience of rejection that profoundly alters our sense of self, usually in childhood, we make a decision about ourselves that separates us from the truth of who we are. This is the **turn from truth**. We unwittingly solidify a negative self-belief as a way to look out for and avoid future situations in which we could experience that pain again.

- This solidification of pain and fear creates the **split self**. And the ensuing negative self-beliefs muddy up our ability to know that **we are already complete**.

- The resulting dissonance is the birth of our **inner opposition**, the internal tug of war that holds us back from joy, possibility, and freedom.

- To manage our inner opposition and quell the discomfort, we develop and continually fine-tune **survival mechanisms** to keep from being found out. Each in our own unique ways, we seek situations, experiences, and accomplishments that prove us as worthy, and we avoid situations that could expose our biggest fear as true. All this seeking and avoiding maps back to rejection, which is equal to the threat of death to the human brain.

The result of these interwoven beliefs, strategies, patterns, and behaviors is what I call the unwinnable quest to prove ourselves and buy our way into feeling peaceful, fulfilled, joyful, and complete. But this is the big trap! You are already seated in your self, and there is simply no amount of evidence that will *ever* accomplish the authentic feeling that completeness really is.

THE PARADIGM OF BELIEF

So let's deconstruct this unwinnable quest and the way that seeking proof of our worth is intimately tied to this quest.

When you turned away from truth and adopted an erroneous negative belief about yourself, your sense of self entered into the paradigm of *belief*. You've heard about beliefs all your life. You've used the word and its derivations countless times. At face value, beliefs are harmless enough. But here is where the problem lies: beliefs naturally require *conditions*.

Why is this problematic? Let me explain.

Inherent in a belief is the possibility that its converse is true. For example, if I believe it's a nice day, you might look out the window and believe that it's not a nice day. As a belief forms, its polar opposite or contrasting belief naturally comes along for the ride. For this reason, the alleged belief needs conditions to validate it and uphold it against its antithesis. I would never assert that "I believe it's a nice day" without anything to back it up. I make the statement because of the data points—the conditions—I've quickly amassed on the topic: there's not a cloud in the sky, there is a soft breeze, and people are out sunning on the park green. In other words, for me, these conditions are necessary for my belief to be in existence.

And it doesn't stop there. I need these conditions to uphold it against any assertion of its opposite. For example, if you were from Antarctica, you might look out the window at the same scene I'm looking at and say, "Are you kidding me? This is way too hot. It's 88 degrees out there! This is absolutely miserable!" The conditions you observe are the following: there is no cloud cover to shield you from the hot sun, the breeze isn't cool enough, and there is no way you'd lay out and cook in the sun like that on the park green.

Needing everything to line up (the conditions) in order to validate your beliefs and uphold it against its converse is the trap! Nowhere is this more poignant than when you consider your sense of self—and your relationship with yourself. When your sense of self is placed in the paradigm of belief, how you perceive yourself becomes *conditional*. You require conditions to validate your worthiness and prove yourself complete.

The reason this is an *unwinnable* quest is because of the nature of proof itself. The moment I need proof to validate my enough-ness, I'm going to be dead set on looking for all the conditions that validate the belief that "I'm good enough," and all in an effort to stay safe from the pain of rejection. And the moment I attempt to tie my worth to certain externals—such as getting accepted into the right college, having the right friends, making a certain sum of money, and otherwise doing whatever I can to win approval and avoid negative judgment from others—then I will equally bump up against all the conditions that validate the opposite. Those counterconditions are things like being passed up for a promotion, not getting asked to lead a high stakes project you're invested in, obsessing over certain friends who make more money than you, being ghosted by the guy you made a great connection with online, not getting invited to a party, or not having all the answers the executive team might ask after your presentation. This is the nature of proof: in the same way you can't see light without dark, you can't see proof unless its contrast makes it evident.

> *The constant assertion of belief*
> *is an indication of fear.*
>
> —JIDDU KRISHNAMURTI

With contrasting evidence always available, inner opposition has you worrying that your negative self-belief will eventually be discovered and proven as true. Commensurate to the amount of proof you seek to prove yourself complete is a collection of evidence, opportunities, and reasons you're working just as hard to avoid. In the paradigm of belief, contrasting proof *feeds* your need to prove. In the never-ending process of proving, you're on an unwinnable quest for just the right conditions, perpetually keeping you from the sense of completeness you so desperately crave.

This is an exhausting and futile attempt at wholeness because your worthiness is not, and never will be, conditional. However, when your sense of self is rooted in the paradigm of belief, you're convinced that you just have to work harder and get *more* proof, "With just that right next set of conditions (the lover, money, job, fitness level, new passport stamp, etc.), I'll *finally* feel settled, content, and fulfilled. I'll finally feel complete." Excuse the cliché here, but if this represents your own internal dialogue, you're barking up the wrong tree.

YOUR WORTHINESS REQUIRES NO VALIDATION

While it may be fun and satisfying to acquire proof—like the "I just landed the biggest deal of my entire career!" kind—it's *not* the reason you are good enough, worthy, or complete. Not to say we shouldn't be appreciating validation or enjoying accolades—not at all. There is no thrill like the thrill of hard-earned accomplishment. Riding the high of a big win is the fruit of the creative process! However, there is a fine line between praise and proof. Because we're hardwired to belong, we have a fundamental need to seek acknowledgment and validation from others. It's natural, it's normal, and it's A-OK to appreciate confirmation that you're on the right track. Revel in your wins and bask in the delight of praise. Just don't mistake it as *evidence* of your worthiness. Praise means nothing about your worthiness. It's simply feedback that you're doing great things and what you're up to is working. Enjoy the praise but don't conflate it as proof. Otherwise, you'll stay trapped on the wild roller-coaster ride that is the paradigm of conditions and beliefs—with big ups and terrifying downs. This is the ride that you can stay on for *years*, convinced that *more* proof or the *right* next set of conditions will finally free you from the search.

Speaking of feedback, if you receive input, information, or criticism that you're off the mark—for example, someone is upset with your approach and thinks that others don't feel safe with your communication style—then take note and recalibrate your behavior. Constructive feedback isn't evidence that your false belief is true, but it's worthy of consideration. Feedback illuminates blind spots. When done well, it works to ensure that the repercussions of your actions are congruent with the intentions you hold. You have impact on others and the world, and that fact is one to be celebrated. You want your words and actions to make a positive difference to your family, friends, colleagues, and community. If you get feedback that they're not, take note. But don't let the feedback take you down. It's information, not evidence.

Choosing to know your worthiness as a human being—just as you are right now—converts praise and criticism from evidence to information. When that shift happens, you stop silently measuring yourself against other people and outer circumstances. You stop competing and comparing in the quest for proof of your value, and you step into a new world of possibility unshackled by fear. Exercising your power to choose is the life-changing factor.

LEARNING HOW TO EXERCISE CHOICE IN A NEW WAY

I will admit that learning to exercise choice in a whole new way can be a bit disorienting at first, especially when you're choosing to understand and know yourself at the deepest level. I'll show you what I mean.

You've come to a door. You *want* to walk through this door. You're *determined* to walk through this door. And so you push against the door. Hard. It budges a little bit, but not nearly enough to slip through. All your life you've walked through doors that open fairly easily when you push them, but for some reason, what normally works isn't working on *this* door. And so you push even harder, but to no avail. Then all of a sudden it hits you, "Oh my gosh, *pull!*" After a small, incredulous chuckle, you're relieved that it was a lot easier than you thought, and you catalog that muscle memory for when you're at another challenging door. You also cut yourself some slack because you were just doing what you were *used* to doing.

Discovering a new or different choice like that feels like an aha moment, like a revelation of expanded awareness. The aha required to employ the kind of effort and perceptual muscle to claim the ultimate choice—which is choosing to know yourself as unconditionally whole and complete—can be as simple (and obvious) as *pulling* the door open.

In truth, this entire book is designed to help you expand your perceptual skills and your awareness at the same time—both of which will aid you in exercising choices to embody a life of joy, clarity, courage, fulfillment, and freedom. And you'll have this new muscle memory forever. But to practice it, you'll have to understand the profound difference between the paradigm of believing and the paradigm of knowing.

The Paradigm of Knowing

Being trapped in the paradigm of belief is akin to pushing harder on the door that's not budging. It's time to wake up to the magic of "pull"—a brand-new approach to how you see and feel about yourself.

On the other side of the split self, which is seemingly trapped in the paradigm of belief, is the complete self that lives in the paradigm of *knowing*. Knowing and believing are very different experiences. Think about some of the things you know, unequivocally. You might know that you have a kind heart, or you might know that you'll always figure it out, no matter what "it" is. Think about all the times you've responded with "I just know that," and notice that it was a *choice* to claim that knowing in that moment, regardless of the conditions. When we choose to know something, it is often a choice that's not validated by a collection of evidence. What's also important to point out here is that *knowing* is an assertion that is almost always unconditional. Let me give you a few examples.

If you're a parent, you might choose to know that your children love you—even when they get angry at you, and yell convincingly at you that they don't; even though they sometimes completely defy you and refuse to clean their rooms or stay in college or follow the career path you hoped they would. You don't see that stuff as evidence that they don't love you. You know that they do despite them saying otherwise in word or deed. Even more, you *choose to know* this love.

As a son or daughter, you might choose to know that your parents love you—even though they might forget the name of the person you started dating six months ago, or, even worse, forget your birthday. If they fail to make that special phone call or send you a card, you don't take that as evidence that they don't love you. You still choose to know that they do—even after they call a few days too late, and then get in a heated political argument with you and you don't talk for three months. Regardless, you still choose to know they love you.

Here's another angle for putting this knowing in perspective: imagine that you just discovered that the name on your official birth certificate is not the name you thought you were given. At this point in your life, if one of your family members presented this information to you and said, "Actually, Sofia, your real name is not at all what you've thought and what you've been called for the past thirty-five years. It's actually Gertie." Would you respond with, "OK, sure. I guess I'll go by Gertie now." No, you'd say, "Thanks, but no thanks. I know what my name is, and it's not that." Despite the conditions—outer conditions that actually prove your name as something else—you still choose to know otherwise. You know yourself as Sofia and choose to move forward with that knowing. The power of the document that says otherwise, while it may hold an interesting story to be explored, is far eclipsed by the power of choice.

Here's another example: think about what you know about your gender. In my case, I know that I'm female. However you self-identify, think about the cognitive and emotional freedom that comes from knowing it, not believing, it. What do I mean by this? Well, when you *know* your gender identity (meaning, "I know I'm a woman"), not believe it ("I believe I'm a woman"), then you require no proof to validate it to yourself and others or uphold it against the possibility of the converse being perceived. In my case, when I wake up in the morning there is no part of me that is concerned that others might think of me as a man. And there is no part of me that worries that regardless of what I look like or wear, someone might take me for a male. And because I know I'm a woman, if somebody were to come up to me and say, "Amy, I actually think you're a man," I wouldn't be triggered or threatened in the least. I would be genuinely baffled and completely curious about their perception. The reason I'm not triggered by their questioning of my gender is because I don't *believe* I'm a woman, I *know* I'm a woman. Therefore, conditions that say otherwise don't register as evidence that their statement is true. On the other hand, if I *believed* I was a woman, then the dual nature of a belief would have me in the business of ensuring others don't see me as a man. If my gender identity rested within the paradigm of belief, their statement would be triggering for me. Perceptual freedom comes from the unconditional nature of knowing—I don't need to prove or disprove anything about my woman-ness.

If you're thinking, "Well, the conditions of my body determine my knowing, so my knowing is actually conditional," then try this amusing exercise: imagine that aliens abducted you tonight and transformed you into the opposite gender—anatomically, neurochemically, and biologically. They even give you a new name that represents the opposite gender. In the morning you wake up, and—after you stop freaking out about being abducted by aliens—they greet you saying, "Hey, hi. You're the opposite gender now." What would you say in response?

"OK. Sure, I guess, you're right." No! You'd say, "No, I'm not."

Then they'd say, "Yes, you are."

"No, I'm not!" you'd insist.

And they'd respond with, "Yes, you *are!*"

And you fight back with, "No, I'm *not!*"

When it gets to the point where the frustrated and exasperated aliens ask you, "*Why* do you keep saying you're not the gender we're informing you of?" You would say this: "Because I *know* what I am."

You would never respond with the phrase "Because I *believe.*" If you retorted with "I *believe* what I am," then the aliens would shoot right back with, "Aha! Our proof trumps your belief! We win!" With all their "proof" or conditions, such as the anatomical and biological changes, they'd swiftly validate their assertion and negate the strength of your belief. "Because I *believe*" just simply wouldn't cut it, and that's why you'd never say it. You innately know you have to go deeper to the place where the argument stops. You have to claim a *knowing* because knowing is unconditional—and incredibly powerful. That perceptual freedom, not needing to prove or disprove anything about who you know yourself to be, is a freedom most of us take for granted. Over the past few years, the transgender community worldwide has created a heightened awareness of and appreciation for this precious sovereign right.

The Leap of Faith: Know Your Essence

What does all this mean for living on purpose and realizing a life of fulfillment and joy? Well, quite simply, the only thing holding you back from your true self and a life of freedom, joy, well-being, and total aliveness is needing to prove yourself out of the habit of inner opposition. Now that you understand that you are already complete, I'm simply going to ask you to *know* that. Knowing is a deeper level of *chosen* truth. Knowing is freedom. And it's a simple choice. You can make the quantum leap into a paradigm in which conditions don't define you. Choose to know your completeness *unconditionally*—in the same way you know your name, your kind heart, or that your parents love you.

Don't believe it. Don't justify it.

Just choose it. Claim it. Claim the essence you *choose* to be—the essence that arises from truth and love. Your essence may be strength, compassion, creativity, empowerment, presence, or resiliency, for example. Claim your essence for no reason other than that it feels right, true, or wanted. There is nothing else you need to do. Choose it and *be* it. Now, big important point: your asserted claim of wholeness can't be just lip service to yourself. Saying the statement "I choose to know that I'm enough" but not *feeling* its truth is like blowing air through your pursed lips and taking it for a whistle. It's a noble effort, but it's not the desired result. The real deal is when you *feel* the truth in your choice and it's as natural as knowing your name. If you can't feel it just yet, then keep trying until the perceptual aha hits you, like when you realize the need to pull and not push the door open.

As you move forward, I would like you to remember that claiming a knowing of your essence and your competency doesn't guarantee that you're going to knock it out of the park every time you go to bat. For example, knowing your resourcefulness doesn't excuse you from hard work and preparation. Yes, it's always working out for you (Choice #3), and *yes*, there isn't a way things should be (Choice #2), but if there's a way you *want* them, then know your essence and get to work.

Remove the resource strain that inner opposition is, and with the clarity and spaciousness that *knowing* provides, channel all your creative power into manifesting and innovating amazing things for yourself and the world.

Knowing is a choice, a privilege, and a clearing for wisdom and joy to arise. What do I mean by a clearing? When you finally make the choice to know the most important things about yourself and your life, all the other noise quiets down. Any mental and emotional material that's vied for your attention simmers down. The old stories, beliefs, and worries that there's something deficient or wrong with you just can't hold together in the benevolent, loving hurricane that knowing is. And the moment you feel its power is the moment you hear yourself whistle for the first time. Try pulling the door open to a new relationship with yourself, one in which you drop the need to argue, prove, and justify, and just claim the truth of you. It's the easiest thing you'll ever do.

THE CHOICES CHECKLIST

Where we're at in the journey:

- ☐ **Choice #1**: Choose to feel it out, not figure it out

    - ☐ **Process/exercise**: Three Steps for Feeling It Out:
      A Process for Integrating Choice #1 (page 50)

- ☐ **Choice #2**: Choose to know that there is no way things—or
  you—should be

    - ☐ **Process/exercise**: Four Steps to Freedom: A Process for
      Integrating Choice #2 (page 82)

- ☐ **Choice #3**: Choose to know that it's always working out for you

    - ☐ **Process/exercise**: Painting Forward: A Process for
      Integrating Choice #3 (page 99)

- ☐ **Choice #4**: Choose to know that you are already complete

    - ☐ **Process/exercise**: Get in Touch with the Truth: Reflections
      for Integrating Choice #4 (page 156)

Chapter 12

BE INTOLERANT OF FEELING CRAPPY

When you are already in Detroit, you don't
have to take a bus to get there.

—RAM DASS

You're late for a doctor's appointment. In the mad dash to gather your keys and wallet, you find that your phone is missing. Frantic, you run around the house yelling to the members of your household, "Gah! *I just had it!* Does anyone see it anywhere? On the counter? In the bathroom? On my desk?" After a few minutes of searching, you realize it's in your hand.

You're giving directions to your friend as he's driving and you're navigating. "Turn left here," you say. As he begins to turn left you call out, "No! *Left!*" He shoots back, "This *is* left!" With a cringe and a sheepish grin you reply, "Oops. I meant the other left."

You're about to leave a friend's house, and you're looking for your glasses. After a few minutes she asks what you're doing. "My glasses. I can't drive home without them." She replies with a smirk, "Um, you're wearing them."

What's your typical response to situations like these?

If you're like me, you laugh. But what about the deeper things we're looking for, beyond the mundane? To paraphrase the spiritual teacher Gangaji, everything we need or seek is "closer than close." It's hiding in plain sight. That's one of the great cosmic jokes. When I first heard the term "cosmic joke" in my spiritual studies as a teenager, I delighted in the nuanced wisdom of those two words side by side. They spoke of something big, something important, but also something inherently funny—maybe even absurd. When it comes to seeking purpose and meaning, could the biggest cosmic joke of them all be that what we're all really seeking is ourselves?

You are already that which you seek.

So goes the ancient wisdom, a wisdom that many of us have a hard time wrapping our heads around. The famous Zen interpreter for Western audiences, Alan Watts, put it like this: "The meaning of life is just to be alive. It is so plain and so obvious and so simple. And yet everybody rushes around in a great panic, as if it were necessary to achieve something beyond themselves."[1] Case in point: the self-help industry is a multibillion-dollar industry, which proves that we are on a constant search for something—for truth, for purpose, for meaning, and for happiness. But coming back to the cosmic joke, those things can only be realized within you—*as you.* And the more you search the more lost you become. Seems simple enough, right? Maybe *too* simple. Maybe that's why the cosmic joke was unknowingly lost on me in those formative years.

However, although spiritual irony was also (mostly) lost on me at sixteen years old, I at least got that there was something inherently amusing about the counterproductive effort toward enlightenment. Probably because I was consumed by counterproductive attempts myself—I just didn't know it. When I was in high school, I remember coming home

---

1   Alan Watts, *The Culture of Counter-Culture: The Edited Transcripts* (Boston: C. E. Tuttle Company, 1998).

from a weekend meditation retreat completely determined to be the most realized meditator on the planet. I'm not kidding. Committed and driven, I militantly meditated for forty-five minutes at 4:00 a.m. and at 6:00 p.m. every single day for six months. I don't say "militantly" lightly. There was nothing graceful or compassionate about my approach to achieving an equanimous state of consciousness. "I'm going to do this, I'm going to do it *right*, and it's going to *work*."

Looking back, I laugh at myself for my hardcore meditation strategy in the same way I'd laugh if I were to discover the missing twenty-dollar bill that I'd been searching for all day in the back pocket of my jeans that, with a light heart. I have compassion for myself for falling prey to the cosmic joke and for being blind to the fact that it applied to *me*.

My journey through an eating disorder, and the other breakdowns and breakthroughs of my life, led me to realize that my inner opposition stemmed from a single source—a belief that I wasn't good enough. But the eventual eye-opening discovery of that negative self-belief wasn't enough for me to break free. In fact, this discovery had the opposite effect. It kicked me into high gear. The way in which I tackled meditation at sixteen years old was the way I tackled transformation and freedom. "I have to be diligent . . . I have to work *hard* to change my thinking . . . I have to change everything about my ways to overcome this debilitating belief. And *then* I will be free." Paradoxically, my misguided but well-intended approach to personal transformation kept me from the peace and fulfillment I knew was my birthright. Yet despite all my effort, I knew it all still boiled down to choice: *I* was the one continuing to harbor this belief, and *I* was the only one who could do something about it. This conundrum—the awareness of the power of choice merging with my inability to choose otherwise—kept me spiritually hungry and dedicated to find a way out.

Maybe it was "the way out" thinking that held me up in my twenties. I had yet to discover that the only way out was *through*, through my own conceptual delusion that freedom exists in a paradigm where I need to earn and prove that I'm a complete human being. It took me about fifteen more years to truly understand that coming back home to the truth was not something to be gained through *trying*, that it could only be realized through present-moment knowing. *We are already that which we seek.*

Once I discovered the profound difference between *believing* and *knowing*—and chose to *know*, not *believe*, my enough-ness—I found my home in the joy, ease, purpose, and fulfillment that has been my true nature from day one. And that is my invitation to you. The final deliberate choice of an always-on-purpose life is Choice #5: choose to know, not believe, your worth.

THE EASIEST (AND POSSIBLY HARDEST) THING YOU'LL EVER DO

Changing beliefs can feel like hard work. That's why I'm not proposing we change them; we're just going to *not choose* the ones that cause inner opposition. To do so, I'm going to help you put Choice #1 to work: you're going to feel (not figure) out your way to *knowing*. Ready?

Taking a step back, you've got to take the proverbial leap from the paradigm of believing into the paradigm of knowing. In other words, instead of believing that you're either good or not good, enough or not enough, you *choose to know* that you are complete. What does that mean? It means that right now, in this moment, you simply decide to know that you're whole and complete *unconditionally*. You choose to know that you are capable, resilient, resourceful, worthy, deserving, and enough. You simply claim this because . . . guess what? You were all these things the day you were born. You were these things before you turned away from truth and have continued to be these things ever since. However, when you turned away from truth you split your sense of self and simply lost touch with *knowing*. The truth is that you've been whole and complete this whole time. When you choose to know this—*and claim it right now*—you are taking off the glasses and claiming the life you were born to live, right now. This just might be the easiest thing you'll ever do because you just do it—and you *can't* use proof.

You also can't validate it.

You can't find reasons for it.

You can't argue for it.

You can't justify it.

You just *choose* it.

Because you can.

It's so simple and obvious it's annoying. Which is why this may be the hardest thing you'll ever do!

Think about what you're up against. *Knowing* your completeness may be like nothing you've ever done. Think about your age and consider that for a good chunk of those years you've gotten a lot of practice proving your worth inside the paradigm of belief. The moment you put those inner opposition glasses on, your world ceased to be objective, and the stuff of life turned into evidence that validated or invalidated your sense of worthiness. This includes everything you've done or haven't done, accomplished or haven't accomplished, experienced or haven't experienced; it involves your relationships, jobs, travels, educational training, and everything else that has captured your time and attention. The stuff of life by which you've assessed your worthiness of course also includes your wins and setbacks, your triumphs and tragedies, and everything in between those polarities that has mattered to you. Every day in the paradigm of belief you've inadvertently sorted through the conditions of your experience to appear good enough, smart enough, capable, or competent because you've been unknowingly living with a lack-based self-*belief*. Naturally, you've got some strong muscle memory for sorting, sifting, and justifying your worth. For this reason, I'll guarantee that your instincts want you to go find *reasons* to claim your completeness and push harder on that door that won't budge: "Cool, got this. Thanks, Amy. I'm totally going to know I'm whole and complete . . . as soon as I get that promotion."

D'oh!

That "*as soon as* . . ." shot you right back into the paradigm of belief.

No conditions can be used to claim your knowing. The moment you reach for that condition, you're back in the unwinnable quest, keeping you an arm's length from the feeling of completeness that already exists within you. (Cosmic joke, anyone?)

How to Choose Knowing Over Believing: A Process for Integrating Choice #5

Remember when we dove into the nature of inner opposition in chapter 6 and discussed how we often sense that we're holding ourselves back somehow—by not believing in ourselves, courting self-doubt, or worrying that something crappy might be true about ourselves—but we just don't know how to choose otherwise? Well, here it is: it's hopping over to the paradigm of knowing and choosing to *know* your completeness in the same way you know your gender identity, your name, or that your parents or kids love you. Unconditionally.

But heads up—choosing to know yourself as whole and complete is not a switch you find in your psyche, flip, and stay in the paradigm of knowing for all time. You don't pull open the door once and assume it will stay open or think that pulling it open once will take care of all doors forevermore. As the American Tibetan Buddhist Pema Chödrön said, "Remember that this is not something we do just once or twice. Interrupting our destructive habits and awakening our heart is the work of a lifetime."[2] Likewise, choosing to know your wholeness is

---

2   Pema Chödrön, *The Places That Scare You: A Guide to Fearlessness in Difficult Times* (Boulder, CO: Shambhala, 2007).

the work of a lifetime. It's a life practice. Moment by moment, if you claim it, you have the freedom to know, not believe, your enough-ness. Moment by moment, you have the power to choose your authentic life. Because that's when life happens: in this moment and this moment only. It's the only thing that's real. The past is a memory, and the future exists in your imagination. This now-moment is the totality of your life. So every time you unconditionally claim your wholeness *now*, you are realizing the life you were born to live. Now.

Yes, effort is required to claim the life you were born to live, but in no way will it be counterproductive. (In other words, the joke *will not* be on you!) To shift out of the realm of "doing" and into the beingness of freedom, joy, and peace that is your birthright, you'll have to do some of the perceptual work we've discussed throughout the pages of this book. However, this work—or effort—can feel effort*less*. Just follow a few steps with me and you will understand:

Step 1: You're going to feel this out, not figure it out. This means that right now, in this moment, you have to care more about how you feel. Period. From here on out, you have to be more sensitive to your emotional state because it is reflecting back what paradigm you're currently operating in. If you're feeling centered, unburdened, hopeful, clear, compassionate, and present, then you're likely operating from your whole and complete self, so keep going and stay the course. But if not, if instead you're feeling the weight of self-doubt or the discomfort and subtle frenzy of wanting to belong or be perceived favorably, then that's your cue to make the leap. In other words, that's when you use the weighty feeling of inner opposition as your indicator that you're hanging out in the paradigm of belief and that your sense of self is conditional at that moment in time.

Why monitor feeling and not thought? Well, if you've ever heard of the term "monkey mind," it's because our minds are a mess.

As a human being, you know this mental state of affairs well. One moment you're wondering what you should have for lunch, the next you're rehashing a conversation from yesterday and wondering if you focused on the right points, and then, quite unceremoniously, you're telling yourself to take the trash cans out to the street for garbage pickup tomorrow. Thoughts happen without you willing them, and that's why your mental momentum can take you down if you're not careful. When monitoring the totality of your inner dialogue—which includes to-do lists, monologues, arguments, and other flavors of self-talk—it's hard to pick out the voice of inner opposition that's fueling your need to prove your worth. But if you let your feeling be your guide, you have only two things to consider at all times: (1) Are you feeling good and feeling empowered? (2) Or are you feeling constricted and hesitant? In other words, when it's time to check in with yourself, where are you along the following spectrum of emotions?

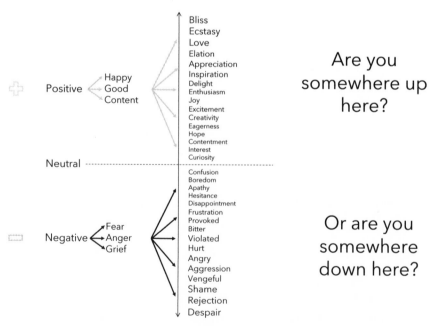

Identifying what side of the neutral line you're on is oftentimes much easier than trying to pinpoint a lack-based belief running in the background of your experience in a moment. After you decide to feel this out and become sensitive to your emotional state, then you're ready for Step 2.

Step 2: Become intolerant of feeling crappy. Think of it this way: If you don't like watching horror films and you turn on the TV one evening, looking forward to kicking back, and up pops a horror film, what do you do? You change the channel. You don't subject yourself to what's on the screen just because it's there. You take control and change it with the (aptly named) remote control in your hand because you don't like the way horror makes you feel. The same goes for your focus. You have the ability to change your perceptual channel and switch from proving your worth to knowing your wholeness with a simple "click" of choice. However, one of the costs of surviving the paradigm of belief for so long is that most of us haven't known that we had that kind of remote control at our disposal. We've been conditioned to the discomfort of inner opposition and the uneasiness of living conditionally. And only because we're desensitized do we fail to recognize that we can change the channel. This is why it's so important to become entirely intolerant of feeling crappy! You have to reorient yourself to feeling good—*really good!* So change the channel as often as you'd like and put your attention on anything and everything that adds to your good feelings.

Step 3: This third and final step I call "catch and come back." When you heighten your sensitivity to the uncomfortable feeling of inner opposition and then catch when life has temporarily pulled you into the paradigm of conditions (because it will!), simply choose to *know* in that moment that you've got this—and come back to truth. Catch yourself in the contraction of a limiting thought or feeling and come back to the truth that you're enough and complete for no other reason than that you simply, *unconditionally*, are. No proof required. Easy!

I liken the feeling of *coming back* to the empowered relief of taking off a VR headset right after you decide that you've had enough of the thrilling threat of angry virtual bees coming after you. Coming back to reality—the reality that you're unconditionally whole—is taking the inner opposition glasses off and seeing yourself, others, and life with clear, *real* eyes. This is when you *realize* that all the power, wisdom, strength, resourcefulness, and resiliency is all right here within you, right now.

And the best part? It's knowing that nothing that happens outside of you (like mistakes, failures, missed opportunities, or setbacks) means anything about your worth, competency, or deservingness. It's just stuff. It's not proof! And so the more you catch and come back to yourself, the freer you are from inner opposition's tragic diatribe of constructive feedback and its litany of so-called evidence. And now you're more energized to powerfully, objectively, and compassionately respond—not react—to any and all experiences you have.

Life is wonderfully rich, full, and compelling. My goodness is it compelling! Its painful and pleasurable surprises unfailingly add to your lived experience—as miraculous, messy, and meaningful as it is. Unless you choose to become a monk in a cave on a mountain, immune from all earthly distractions and the triggering nature of relationships, the stuff of life is going to sideswipe you sometimes. As much as I practice living on purpose, the paradigm of belief can still suck me into its vortex if the situation, interaction, or context is sticky enough. For example, I know that meeting a group of brilliant and fabulously successful and celebrated individuals can set off a tremor of self-doubt, sending voltage to the thought, "I'm not good enough." Because I'm practiced at being intolerant of feeling crappy, I usually catch that tremor pretty quickly and immediately shift to *knowing* my completeness. I catch the old dynamic and come back to my authentic self, where I operate from truth, power, and presence.

If I were to slow down that moment of being pulled by the gravitational weight of the past and put words to my present-moment process, it might sound like this:

Oh, goodness me! There it is—the I'm-not-good-enough worry. Nope! Not gonna happen. In the same way I know I'm a woman, I know I'm whole and complete. Right now. No proof needed. Just because I didn't have an answer to that question doesn't mean anything. Just because I made a mistake doesn't mean anything about my competency. I'm whole and complete. In the same way I know my name, I know I'm enough in this moment, and the stuff of life doesn't mean anything about my worth.

BOOM! Glasses off. And I'm back.

Catching and coming back once might be enough to do the trick, to stay rooted in your whole and complete self for the life of that circumstance. But not always! You might continue to get sideswiped depending on the situation. For example, years ago I remember being in a brainstorming meeting with highly respected thought leaders from around the world. Yeah, a nightmare for my inner opposition and a dream for my true self. Appreciating and playing off their contributions both buoyed my spirit and electrified my fear that I didn't really belong there. Underneath my engaged and seemingly even-handed presence, I had to catch and come back multiple times during the course of that meeting. But I'll tell you, I chuckled to myself every time I did. You too can make a life-affirming game out of catching and coming back. How to make it both fun and effective is what comes next.

FIND YOUR RUMBLE STRIP

As I envision it, somewhere in the distance between your unconditionally whole self and your conditionally false self is an internal rumble strip, much like the rumble strip along the side of a highway— the grooves in the road that alert us when we're potentially heading toward danger.

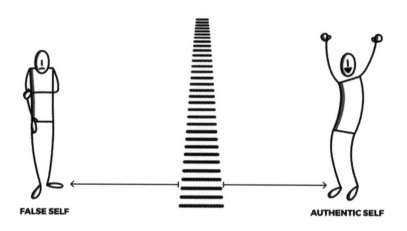

FALSE SELF   AUTHENTIC SELF

In the same way a rumble strip separates the road from the bushes or anything else that lies beyond the shoulder, there is a separator between the real you and the false you. If you've ever had the experience of accidentally veering off the freeway and onto a rumble strip, you know just how jolting and motivating it is to get right back on the road. While it's lovely to have that built-in indicator on our highways, we have to actively create and mind our own rumble strip that separates the paradigm of belief from the paradigm of knowing. If knowing yourself as already whole and complete is a new practice for you, your rumble strip might be pretty close to your false self at this point.

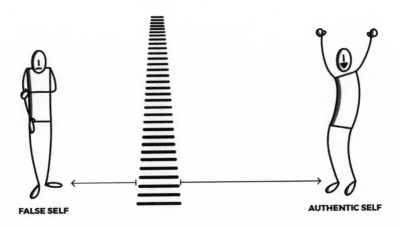

FALSE SELF   AUTHENTIC SELF

This means that for just a little while longer, it might take you really feeling the grip of inner opposition before you realize you can catch and come back. As you practice catching and coming back, you heighten your sensitivity to how you feel and become more intolerant of feeling crappy. Which simply means that your rumble strip gets closer and closer to your authentic self. You begin to feel the pull toward self-doubt and other limiting emotions more quickly, sensing subtle vibrational changes before veering astray from who you really are. In other words, with your rumble strip resting closer to your authentic self, you're able to quickly reorient into the paradigm of knowing.

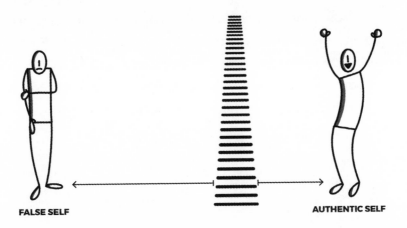

FALSE SELF   AUTHENTIC SELF

This is the benefit of being intolerant of feeling crappy!

Regardless of where your rumble strip is right now, don't ever be hard on yourself for catching yourself in the grips of your false self and inner opposition. Get excited for the false-self/authentic-self duality that allows you the thrill of choice—the thrill of choosing freedom. Can you imagine if you floated along without the chance to wake up from false perception and come back to truth? Claiming, in a moment, the life you want and were born to live is what it's all about! I believe this is why humans are in embodied form, and why we develop with a primal need to belong and take on subtle and not-so-subtle false beliefs in the process of navigating through life with others. It's all to have the opportunity to experience who we aren't so that we have the privilege to claim who we *really* are. And to *live*. On purpose.

When you claim the truth of you in a moment, you perceive through clear eyes, and you have no fear. Once you know how to make the leap, then everything you're up to is rooted in truth and love. Free of trying to prove your worth, you genuinely fall in love with life. Creating a vibrant vision of your future is no longer about creating a five-year plan; it becomes a continual practice in being present, appreciative, and choosing what feels good, creative, and life-giving—moment by moment. Living always on purpose is not about finding a continuous state of knowing and staying there. It's a life practice where you choose to care about how you feel, appreciate when you're clear and grounded in unconditional wholeness, and choose to come back to it when you catch that you're not. Becoming proficient at this will be one of the most fulfilling and joy-inducing skills you will ever learn.

THE CHOICES CHECKLIST

Where we're at in the journey:

- ☐ **Choice #1**: Choose to feel it out, not figure it out
    - ☐ **Process/exercise**: Three Steps for Feeling It Out: A Process for Integrating Choice #1 (page 50)
- ☐ **Choice #2**: Choose to know that there is no way things—or you—should be
    - ☐ **Process/exercise**: Four Steps to Freedom: A Process for Integrating Choice #2 (page 82)
- ☐ **Choice #3**: Choose to know that it's always working out for you
    - ☐ **Process/exercise**: Painting Forward: A Process for Integrating Choice #3 (page 99)
- ☐ **Choice #4**: Choose to know that you are already complete
    - ☐ **Process/exercise**: Get in Touch with the Truth: Reflections for Integrating Choice #4 (page 156)
- ☐ **Choice #5**: Choose to know, not believe, your worth
    - ☐ **Process/exercise**: How to Choose Knowing Over Believing: A Process for Integrating Choice #5 (page 204)

Chapter 13

MAGIC WITHOUT FANFARE

Over time, you will form an intensely personal relationship
with this beautiful inner force. It will replace the relationship
you currently have with inner pain and disturbance.
Now peace and love will run your life.

—MICHAEL A. SINGER, *THE UNTETHERED SOUL*

"It's a big deal. But it's not really that big of a deal. I've changed, yet nothing is really different. I feel lighter. And clearer. Even my husband has noticed a shift. By no means am I perfect or 'done,' but I feel free. Like I'm finally living my truth. It's so simple and obvious. Yet it's really profound. It's a paradox, for sure."

This is what Kim told me in one of our later coaching sessions. She had officially made the leap from the paradigm of belief to the paradigm of knowing about eight weeks prior. Learning about the split self was a big turning point for her in our work together. The moment Kim understood the source of her battling inner dialogues—one voice believing in her competency and the other one doubting her worth— she was able to make the shift to *knowing* herself as complete. Actively choosing to operate from her core self, unconditionally, Kim removed the existential crisis she had been mired in and made available a power and presence she had never embodied before. She spent the eight weeks prior to our session practicing the ability to advocate for herself more powerfully and framing challenges as welcome contrast instead of unwanted threats. Happily reflecting on what life and work felt like without inner opposition in the driver's seat, Kim accurately captured the mellow magic of her transformation.

I say "mellow" because awakening to your unconditional wholeness clears your path of drama. In the space once consumed by inner opposition resides a calm clarity, peaceful presence, and meaningful joy. What emerges is time and energy. That's magic. Magic without fanfare. Which is both a big—and not-so-big—deal. Why? Because, after too much struggle and pain, you're finally stepping into the life you were born to live, the life your soul has known and held a torchlight for since the day you were born.

But your heart has known it too. And your mind has probably had an inkling of the possibility. It's just been impossible to figure out how to be free in the paradigm of belief. And rightfully so, because we can't *figure* ourselves into this transformation! So instead, let's honor those knowings and follow the inklings by embracing five extraordinary choices.

Summarizing the Five Deliberate Choices to Realize Fulfillment and Joy

Choice #1: Choose to feel it out, not figure it out.

Your soul is speaking to you through the language of inspiration. Listen to your mind but follow your heart. It knows the truth. This journey transcends the intellect and aligns your most expansive inklings, inspirations, and knowings to the path of least resistance, which is the path of most abundance, which is the expression of your best life. And while there is no *absolute* path to find or formula to follow, this is your unique journey, which you alone get to create. To do that you must . . .

Choice #2: Choose to know that there is no way things—or you—should be.

Drop the word "should" from your vocabulary and notice how much easier life is when you let go of this idea that there is some imaginary standard you need to adhere to. There is no big book handed down from the sky that details all the things you must do to live the good life. Release the weight of "should" and focus only on what you *want* and what is true. You can do that when you . . .

Choice #3: Choose to know that it's always working out for you.

Even when it doesn't seem like it! Why entertain anything else? Recognize the fertilizer that each manure moment is and focus on the blossoms that will inevitably sprout in your life. Powerful growth comes from the contrast life provides, so honor and appreciate the opportunity to know what you don't want so you can know what you do want. Honor the opportunity to know who you aren't so you can claim who you are. Now, how do you do that?

Choice #4: Choose to know that you are already complete.

You always have been, and you always will be. Have compassion for yourself for having taken on a few wonky beliefs in order to stay safe from rejection. Be easy on yourself for being practiced in surviving them. Knowing your completeness is a moment-by-moment practice, not a one-time decision for all time. Have fun with it. Don't demonize your split self when you find yourself entertaining a false belief. It happens to all of us! Instead, get excited for the chance to choose truth again, and again . . . and again. Even when it's hard. And when it is *really* hard . . .

Choice #5: Choose to know, not believe, your worth.
Believing requires proof. There is no amount of evidence that will ever prove yourself complete. Knowing your truth is a choice in claiming your worth. Unconditionally. Knowing is a choice. Once you *choose* to know your worth unconditionally, it's just so.

All good things take time. Giving birth to a new thought, action, habit, and even a new life requires a gestation period. You've been in a gestation period. Living with inner opposition has developed within you a determination to break free from false perception. Has that determination lead you to decide it's time for a metamorphosis? If life has led you to that decision, now is the time to act—to *choose*. These five choices are your pivotal moment of change.

LIFE AFTER THE LEAP

Many of us wish for significant change in our lives. We buy the books, sign up for the seminars and retreats, hire trainers and coaches, and enlist mentors to keep us accountable to the change we so desperately seek. Some of us succeed and some of us don't. But if we don't, it's usually not for a lack of trying. It's more often an unwillingness to get uncomfortable and continue the new life practice when it feels awkward. The author Seth Godin says, "True learning (as opposed to education) is a voluntary experience that requires tension and discomfort."[1] That's also true for growth and transformation. Transformation

---

1   Seth Godin, *The Practice* (New York: Portfolio Penguin, 2020).

is voluntary. It requires that we choose it—choose it and choose it and choose it again despite the discomfort. If we're not quick to give up on ourselves, then we've got a real shot!

Making new choices and shifting your perception at a foundational level isn't hard, but it does take practice, time, and self-compassion. It takes some effort, for sure. But it's worth it. And as you incorporate the five choices and make them your own, you won't be making garden variety choices; you'll be making life-changing choices.

But you don't have to take my word for it. Following is a conversation with one of my clients, Meghan. Meghan is an executive of a large Fortune 500 technology company, and through our work together she is now living and leading on purpose. In the hopes of getting you excited about your life after the leap, Meghan agreed to share her transformation.

Me: Meghan, you've said doing this work has changed your life. What exactly is different?

Meghan: I've become comfortable in my skin. I think and act from my truth. I'm free.

Me: What does that mean in your day-to-day life? Can you give me some examples?

Meghan: I can. One example is that I've decided this year, I'm going to be the girl who says The Thing—the thing that everyone else is afraid to say. I'm going to say it nicely, but I'm going to say the thing that everybody else is wanting to say but is just too scared to. Why? Because it's no longer about *me*. It's about my team. It's about the health of the business. My community. My family. Because it's no longer about me, I'm not afraid anymore. My life and focus are bigger than me now. And so that's where the comfort in my skin comes from. I know that I'm competent enough most of the time, that it's working out most of the time, so it's OK to be honest and authentic.

Me: What I'm essentially hearing is that you've come to know your enough-ness so much that there is no threat to that. You know what's inherently true about you so there is no need to protect your image or prove your worth. Did I get that right?

Meghan: Yes, and it's not just at work. It's showing up in every aspect of my life. I've gotten to a point where I know I'm a good leader at home, for sure. I know I'm a good leader at work. Now I'm starting to ask myself, how am I a good leader in my community? It's OK to speak up and take a stand for something bigger than me in other aspects of my life as well.

Me: What's allowed you to do that?

Meghan: Honestly, being strong and secure in my core values and what I stand for. In the beginning of the pandemic we were all navigating without a map. There were hard things about work, about life, and about how we all showed up every day. I remember sitting down, feeling so overwhelmed, feeling like I was failing at everything. In that moment, I decided that whenever I didn't know what to do, I was going to go back to my core values and start there. For me my core values are gratitude, honesty, and family. Literally, that meant starting each decision based on what was working and being grateful for how we were all going to get through it together. For honesty, it meant I was always going to speak honestly when I didn't know what we were doing, when we were going to take a leap without knowing if there was a net, and when I was scared. And finally, I was going to publicly prioritize my family and my team's families. I learned during the COVID pandemic that we are all 100 percent replaceable at work, and 0 percent replaceable at home. And being public about how I include and prioritize my family gave my team permission to do the same with their families.

Me: How do you do that daily?

Meghan: It's not a *try* or a *do*, it's just a way of being now. In the beginning it was a series of continual choices and reminding myself that making those choices is how I tap into my truth. Living and leaning into my stance and my values created a grounding for me. Also, revisiting our work, keeping the conversation going with you, and allowing some time to adjust to a new way of perceiving myself are all the things that made it stick. After enough time of shifting my worry about what people thought of me to actually focusing on what is most important—my family, my team, the health of the business—it's now just who I am . . . most often.

Me: Speaking of others, can you tell me how you relate to others differently now?

Meghan: I'm more empathetic. Because I can see other people's stories and the glasses they're looking through in a way I couldn't before. I mean, not all the time, but I can usually very clearly artic-ulate to somebody how to reframe a situation because I empathize with who they really are. I can help them out of their distress and that is incredibly rewarding.

Me: Put another way, the moment you know your wholeness and completeness you can see it in everybody else. And so you see very objectively the world others create from their own fears, false beliefs, and perception of reality. And you see it with compassion.

Meghan: Yes. Exactly. But in the beginning I had to check myself. I had to tell myself to stop worrying about "my brand" and start worrying about my team. That took work. When I was worried about myself, I couldn't actually feel for them because I was busy feeling for me. But now, it's not "I," it's "we." There's nothing to worry about anymore when it comes to "me" because I genuinely know I'm enough. That's why it's not about me anymore. It's about them. I *genuinely* want what's best for them. Because I don't need to prove my own significance anymore, there is so much room for other people.

Me: Talk to me about validation and proof.

Meghan: That's the biggest shift. But it's not that I stopped looking for validation, I still enjoy that! Who doesn't like a good compliment? But it's different, it's information now. It's not proof. I've removed my self-worth from the situation and use validation as feedback.

Me: Tell me more.

Meghan: Well, now when I get feedback—the good, the bad, and the ugly—I first check whether it feels true to me. I can do that now because I *know* myself. Feedback is information, not evidence. So it's not triggering. I'm able to meet it all objectively and then act powerfully and compassionately.

Me: How does that make your life better?

Meghan: It's a lot less drama! I'm not striving as much and what results is energy. I've released the toxic energy that comes with prolonged stress, which has freed up a ton of time, space, and energy.

Me: What do you do with all that time, space, and energy?

Meghan: I give it back. I spent so much time and energy seeking approval that I now get to give it back without an extra tax on my work–life balance. I now have it to share.

Me: And that feels . . .?

Meghan: Impactful. Meaningful.

Me: Like the life you were born to live?

Meghan: Oh my god, if you told me years ago that the life I was born to live would include being a leader in marketing enterprise software, I'd be like, "I don't even know what that is! Nor do I even care!" But I love my profession now in a way that I couldn't have foreseen, because first and foremost I love who I work with (which is easier when it's not about you). No matter what position I hold, I know that I'm truly living as the best version of myself. Living my best life starts with knowing myself as enough before I even get out of bed in the morning.

Me: What would you want others to know about living their best self? About making the on-purpose choices we've worked with throughout our time together?

Meghan: I would say, you will get more time and have more energy when you stop striving for validation and approval. You'll have deeper and more meaningful relationships because other people will know who you are. And they'll trust that *you* know who you are. You'll have an ability to speak up and to do so with conviction. Whether that's in your school district, in your town, or in your job, you'll have a platform for speaking the truth. Because you'll know *your* truth. And the best part? You won't actually care if others agree. Sure, it'd be nice if they did! But it won't mean anything about your worth if they don't. Then you become so much more involved in your own life. You have impact you want to have. And even better, you *create* impact. Best of all, you feel more alive and free.

Me: Because the stuff of life—like successes and setbacks, accomplishments and disappointments—is just stuff now. Not proof.

Meghan: It's just stuff. Yes, that's how I would describe it.

Me: Anything else?

Meghan: Yes. You know you are yourself when it's not hard.

Me: And when you're yourself, you experience this incredibly rich, teeming-with-possibility spaciousness where presence, joy, and gratitude emerge.

Meghan: Yep. Life is just easier.

Me: Yeah. Totally. It's just easier.

Meghan will be the first to admit that this is a journey. Sometimes the road loops back and you have to reground yourself in order to move forward.

But Meghan ultimately broke through the age-old belief that has caused untold suffering in our world—that growth, accomplishment, achieving anything worthwhile, and generally living a great life requires that we work hard. That we bust our butts to make more, prove more, and attain more. She boldly stepped out of that painful and consuming paradigm—she got off the roller-coaster approach to conditional living—and now enjoys the mellow magic of more time and energy in her life; of more meaning, joy, and impact. And you can too. Life after the leap is worth it. You can make it happen starting right now. One deliberate choice at a time.

THE CHOICES CHECKLIST

Where we're at in the journey:

☐ **Choice #1**: Choose to feel it out, not figure it out

    ☐ **Process/exercise**: Three Steps for Feeling It Out:
A Process for Integrating Choice #1 (page 50)

☐ **Choice #2**: Choose to know that there is no way things—or you—should be

    ☐ **Process/exercise**: Four Steps to Freedom: A Process for Integrating Choice #2 (page 82)

☐ **Choice #3**: Choose to know that it's always working out for you

    ☐ **Process/exercise**: Painting Forward: A Process for Integrating Choice #3 (page 99)

☐ **Choice #4**: Choose to know that you are already complete

    ☐ **Process/exercise**: Get in Touch with the Truth: Reflections for Integrating Choice #4 (page 156)

☐ **Choice #5**: Choose to know, not believe, your worth

    ☐ **Process/exercise**: How to Choose Knowing Over Believing: A Process for Integrating Choice #5 (page 204)

You now have all the tools for the
deliberate practice of living on purpose.

It's time to ease into mellow magic.

Chapter 14

THE ART OF LIVING

Today is the only day available to us today, and we can
take good care of it. That is why today is so important—
the most important day of our lives. Have a good day
today. This is not only a wish. But a practice.

—THICH NHAT HANH

If you had nothing to prove, if no part of you needed validation from others to feel a sense of meaning or purpose, how would you spend your time? What would motivate you to succeed and do well? Without the need to justify your worth or elevate your image for the sake of belonging or admiration, would you be driven to excel? To make change in the world? To make a difference in the lives of others?

Sure you would!

But to get to the heart of your answers, you have to understand that each one of these questions is a matter of focus and priorities. If your focus is no longer rooted in the paradigm of belief, then the questions naturally evolve to, "Well then, what are my priorities? Where do I place my attention, and for what reason?"

You have so far learned that feeling it out (as opposed to figuring it out) is the on-purpose way to answer the big questions. Namely, because there is no guidebook (aka *The Big Book of Shoulds*) to adhere to. When you let your feeling be your guide, you choose the most life-giving, least resistant option—the most expansive and inspiring thought, word, or behavior—as often as you can remember to do so. You do this because it's all about a feeling anyway. You, me, and everyone else on the planet just wants to feel good.

So feeling your way to feeling good is the answer to, *What do I focus on?*

But there isn't a one-size-fits-all approach to feeling good! Knowing what you now know about inner opposition, let's review what it means to feel good.

FROM BELIEF TO RELIEF

As you now know, when you're hanging out in the paradigm of belief, which is a cognitive framework of conditions, it means that your sense of self, in that moment, is conditional. The voice of belief can be encapsulated like this: *in order to be this kind of person, I need to have, know, accomplish, achieve, buy, or be endowed with that.* This habituated way of thinking happens to me, it happens to you, it happens to the best of us. Of course there is nothing inherently wrong with wanting conditions to feel good, but when we *require* them to feel good and to feel complete, then joy is fleeting, frenetic, and unsustainable.

Why?

Because there is no number of conditions that will ever equate to the feeling that unconditional completeness truly is. It's easy to ignore the fact that the temporary thrill we feel from achieving conditions isn't actually from the conditions themselves. In reality, conditions (such as 400 likes on your last Instagram post, getting a job offer, landing a date with your secret crush, or buying a Hermes Birkin bag) temporarily abate the persistent discomfort of inner opposition. The lessening of that resistance results in relief. Which feels good. It's the releasing of inner opposition, not the conditions themselves, that makes us feel good for a little while. But—and this is a big *but*—we're immediately onto the next bigger and better thing.

When you close this book, one of the things I most want you to remember—what I invite you to scribble onto pieces of paper and distribute throughout your world—is this:

> When you *know* yourself as whole and complete,
> then you are already living in unconditional joy, love, and
> fulfillment.
> When you *know* yourself as whole and complete,
> you experience a profound quality of presence and peacefulness,
> and there is nothing more to *want* in order to feel better.

Sure, you can want things—like a bigger house, another dog, or a different hairstyle—and you *will* want things. But the reasons will no longer be about making you feel more complete. You now want it because it's fun. Not required. In unconditional wholeness, inner opposition isn't operational, so it can't motivate you to prove, accomplish, or attain more so that you'll feel worthy—temporarily. Temporarily is no longer good enough. You're free from the unwinnable quest and the trap of short-lived happiness, and now true happiness is here.

You're already complete. Which *is* the best feeling.

It's your life as it has been, just without the drama.

It's relief.

You are free to navigate life and create from a place of clarity, love, and service. Your reason for wanting is not to fill a hole. Your focus broadens beyond you (more on this in a moment).

Everything feels possible.

And nothing feels urgent and filled with anxiety.

So if nothing feels urgent and everything is possible, where else do you put your focus? Do you look ahead and strategize your year? Do you set New Year's resolutions? Do you map out a ten-year plan to launch a new business to make seven figures? Sure! But only if it feels expansive and it comes from inspiration. *And* if you are clear that you are thinking, speaking, and acting from unconditional wholeness. Not from fear, where you're endlessly seeking justification and validation.

However, it's important to clarify again that fear is not your enemy. Far from it. Fear is a reliable indicator of the lens of perception you're looking through. When you begin to regard fear as a friend that is giving you a loving wake-up call—letting you know when you're in relationship with yourself in a way you really don't intend—then you are empowered to consciously redirect your focus.

The ability to direct and redirect your focus truly is a bona fide superpower. One of the keys to claiming this superpower is to become ruthlessly honest and clear about your underlying objective in any given moment—the objective that may or may not be the purpose or goal you've stated verbally or written down. It may not be the intention you *think* you're operating from when you first ask yourself, *What is my ultimate objective here?* Sometimes you've got to dig deeper.

The Direct Path to Mastery: Knowing What You Stand For

We've all been sold a bill of goods when it comes to achievement and worldly success. It's drilled into our collective ethos that *effort* is king. In truth, *focus* is king.

At every moment in time each and every one of us has a primary, underlying objective for the actions we take. For example, as I am writing these words on this page, my ultimate underlying objective *could* be to prove my point of view to you, *or* it could be to ultimately impress you, *or* to get you to like me as an author, *or* it could be to convince the skeptics, *or* it could be to empower you to freedom and possibility. There are many lenses through which to view our motivation, but *one* lens always wins out as the primary objective. (In this case, I'm all about empowering you, and I'm intentionally and deliberately choosing that!)

Check this out for yourself. Notice what is true for you as you read this book. Your ultimate underlying objective might simply be to finish it, *or* to be entertained by new ideas, *or* to pass the time, *or* to unlock the ability to live your best life. You may have several reasons and goals propelling you to read it, but are you aware of what that primary objective, or lens, is right now? Are you intentionally choosing it, or is it just happening?

Most of the time, that primary objective just happens without our deliberate choosing. In my coaching work, I tend to speak about this reality as a *stance* we're (unknowingly) holding. Put another way, in each moment in time we're standing for something—meaning that we have deemed something to be of primary importance and meaning, and we've aligned our purpose with it. The very real challenge is that we're often not aware of what we're really standing for. For example, think of a time when you were in an argument with a partner, spouse, or co-worker and reflect on what your ultimate underlying objective (or stance) was. Your noble self would like to think you were standing for harmony or efficiency or doing the right thing or both of you having a successful outcome, and that is what caused you to have such a strong point of view. It's why you fought for it. "If you just saw it my way, this wouldn't be an issue, and we'd be in a good place right now." But nope: if you were really honest with yourself, you weren't standing for mutual success—you were likely standing for being right or winning or saving face in some way. Disagreements escalating into arguments is often a reliable sign that one or both people have their heels dug into their internal position—to their stance.

An unacknowledged stance and the objective it's built on is running in the background in every moment. It's easy to assume we're always standing for the noble thing that serves the highest good for each situation. Why? Because we know we have good intentions! We want to live and let live! We want to love and be loved! But there is more to the story. Without realizing it, we often default into a constricted I-centric stance: being right over being connected, proving a point over co-creating solutions, avoiding conflict over giving real feedback, being liked over being bold.

As you begin to pierce through these patterns with your growing awareness, shedding light on these underlying drivers and using the understanding that comes from that to redirect your focus accordingly, you will find yourself choosing to be bold over being liked more often than not—and in so many areas of your life. How good will *that* feel?

We're All in Front of the Room at a Point in Time

My work as a public speaking and executive presence coach is one of the most exhilarating parts of my professional life. There is nothing like public speaking—or just the *thought* of public speaking—to bring to the surface everything we've explored throughout this book. Every fear of who we think we are and who we think we are not. And every strategy we've ever learned to manage those fears.

As you begin to work with this material, your boldest, bravest self comes to the front of the room, so to speak. You begin to walk and talk and feel like yourself again—fully self-expressed—like the whole and complete you. But on occasion, you also experience the challenges of old ways of being. Fear. False beliefs. This being the case, think back to the last time you were gripped by nervousness because all eyeballs were on you.

In preparing for your moment in the spotlight, let's look at the challenges you're most apt to face. Almost every client of mine tells me something like this: "The moment I have to speak I become a wreck—my hands start sweating, my heart starts racing, my breathing becomes shallow, I hear a high-pitched ringing in my ears. Next thing I know the presentation is over. Everyone says I did fine, but I can't imagine that's true. How do I get rid of my nervousness?"

Despite their accomplishments—like having majored in communications, or being a whiz at speech writing, or knowing the company's messaging like the back of their hand—what stumps them all is that despite their formidable talents and gifts, they still get nervous when they have to speak up in front of others. To unwind from this, it's important to first make a distinction between *nerves* and *nervousness*: nerves are healthy and normal. Nervousness is manufactured and unnecessary.

When it comes to speaking in front of people, especially people you're not familiar with, you're going to get a surge of nerves. That's healthy, that's normal, that's *wanted*. It's adrenaline, and you don't want to resist that surge. Think of that surge as a power source for you to channel into your message and connect with your audience.

When we don't realize that nerves are a normal part of the process, we can push against that biological phenomenon, and the sheer act of resisting adrenaline can take you down and be easily mistaken as anxiety. Nervousness is a different ballgame altogether. Nervousness is a symptom. Yes, a symptom of fear, but it runs deeper than that. Nervousness is the result of an unacknowledged stance that isn't serving you in that moment. Without fail, nervousness means that, in that moment, you are actually standing for looking good, proving yourself, protecting your image, or gaining admiration.

In other words, *you are standing for you.*

You are *not* standing for the reason you are speaking in the first place! Which could be urgency, connection, possibility, or something else. There's a purpose to that message and the truth is you're not at all aligned with that purpose, that objective, that stance. Instead, you've (unintentionally) made it all about proving yourself in that moment.

Proving!

You can again use fear (nervousness) as an indicator that you've slipped into the paradigm of belief. You can also use it as an indicator that your primary objective has shifted to proving yourself. Which now we know how counterproductive that is! In a state of proving, all your internal bandwidth is jammed up and preoccupied with how you're being perceived and made unavailable for eloquence, wit, and responding to your audience powerfully.

When it comes to life in general, standing for your *self* steals away resources for being connected, peaceful, free from inner opposition, and in service to something greater. Here's the truth:

It's *not* about you and it never will be.

Just as you read about Meghan's transformation in the previous chapter, see what happens when you allow this truth to sink in. See what happens when you remove yourself from the equation, when you get in touch with what's *really* important to you, and when you stand for that.

You might be thinking, "But Amy! There *are* instances in which it *is* about me! What about winning them over in my interview? Or defending my dissertation? Or being scrutinized by the board?" Guess what? You are mistaken. It's not about you. You're already unconditionally whole and complete. Yes, you've got work to do, you've got a job to accomplish, you have an idea to get out into the world, you have an impact to make. Take your inherent worth out of the equation and get clear about what it's really about. It's always bigger than you. Claim *that* stance.

When you practice living from an unconditional *knowing* of (and not believing of) your worth, it follows that all that is left to choose is a stance that goes beyond self. So back to our original question, "What do I focus on now that I'm unconditionally whole and complete?" You claim, moment by moment, a stance that goes beyond proving yourself, staying safe, staying small, being liked, or avoiding conflict. And you claim it in a moment. Over and over. Is it love? It is peace? Is it growth? Is it connection? Is it possibility? Freedom?

Whatever you claim, you'll know it's authentic to you when it's about service. Not self-importance.

Feel this out. How? If you're sensing constriction in your body, fear in your heart, doubt in your mind, worry in your thoughts, then chances are you've slipped over into the paradigm of belief and you're making the moment about you (and staying safe in some way). But never fear, because that's OK! It happens to all of us. We just have to decide we're intolerant of that feeling enough to commit to coming back to a conscious stance—to a knowing, to our truth—that originates in unconditional wholeness; a stance that transcends the self.

As immersed as I am on this topic—talk about it regularly, coach on it often, practice it daily—I *still* have to catch myself! Just the other week, I was in an executive coaching session with a new client. An up-and-coming start-up brought me on board to coach their C-suite to become more conversationally intelligent. On my first call with their chief financial officer, I could feel myself falling into a preoccupation about what he thought about me. *Does he think I'm capable? Is he judging me? Does he like me?* During the first thirty minutes of our conversation, his deadpan expression didn't give me much to go on. I wasn't able to gauge my connection with him as easily as I can with other clients. His lack of expression and minimal dialogue evoked anxiety in me, because remember, our need to be connected is primal! That anxiety was serenading me directly into the paradigm of belief to protect myself and win him over. Luckily, I'm extremely sensitive to the discomfort that a self-stance, such as proving myself, creates. My rumble strip is right off the edge of my knowing, so I catch that discomfort right quick and use it as a cue to come back.

And that is what I did. I caught the uneasiness and came right back to, *Amy! This isn't about proving myself! This is about connection. This is about empowering him to new skills, perspectives, and creating greatness, which will positively impact everyone around him. I'm standing for connection and empowerment. This is not about me.*

And then BOOM! Like something out of a Looney Tunes cartoon, my wandering focus was wrangled right in and shot right back into the center of truth. During our two-hour session, I had to catch and come back at least four times. *Catch and come back. Catch and come back.* That's the practice. Do I judge myself for that? No way. Do I celebrate the opportunity to deliberately choose my stance? Sure do.

Because it's freedom, it's joy, it's impact. And it's me living my life on purpose.

MEDITATION: THE ROYAL ROAD TO ON PURPOSE

Understanding these concepts is one thing, practicing them is something else entirely. Catching inner opposition and coming back to truth is an awareness muscle you need to find and exercise daily. In practice it looks like this:

1. You are sensitive enough to catch when you are standing for your *self* in the paradigm of belief, and . . .

2. You have the internal resources to come back—to choose the paradigm of knowing.

3. Your ability to do these two things successfully depends entirely on your self-awareness. I can't stress this enough.

The quickest and most powerful way to get to the heart of self-aware-ness and be great at these two things is meditation. Why? Think about the act of catch and come back. Where else do we do this in a practice? Meditation, of course! While we sit in meditation, we nonjudgmentally observe a point of focus—whether that's the breath, a candle flame, ambient sounds, or our heartbeat. When we find ourselves lost in thought (which we undoubtedly will) our job is to notice or catch ourselves think-ing, and then lovingly come back to our chosen focus. Every time we catch and come back in meditation it's like doing a bicep curl for the part of the brain that allows us to be meta-aware in our normal waking moments. Meta-aware enough to notice the discomfort of inner opposition so we can do something about it. Meditation heightens our sensitivity to the white noise that is inner opposition. Meditation gives us access to choose a new focus, a new thought, and a new behavior. The more we practice the act of catch and come back in meditation, the stronger and more able we are to notice the subtle changes in our internal state and come back to truth in our daily lives.

If you're not meditating regularly maybe you've tried it at least a few times, figured you're doing it wrong, and have told yourself, *I'll get to that someday.* You might have some "should" energy behind it—you have an inkling that meditating could contribute to a better quality of life, and you tell yourself that you should do it, but you lack the genu-ine desire and discipline to make it a daily practice. If that's the case, I hear you! In all my years of reading, researching, and practicing various forms of mindfulness practices and various forms of meditation, I spent many of those years trying to make meditation a habit. It took many starts and stops, loads of patience, and a few perspective shifts to get on the other side of that effort. I can confidently say now that meditating is such a part of my morning routine that I don't think twice. And I know for sure that this practice is my daily sacred workout that gives me the strength for self-awareness, the power to choose to be always on purpose, and the peace of knowing that I always am.

A SIMPLE MINDFULNESS MEDITATION PRACTICE

The combination of the meditation practice and perspectives I'm about to outline for you has helped many of my clients incorporate meditation as a daily practice. Not because I sell them on the benefits, but instead I clear up enough misconceptions for them to develop the patience and self-compassion to keep the practice going.

Here is a simple three-step practice to try and ways to reframe the obstacles that may hold you back and make meditation a part of your daily routine.

Step 1: Situate yourself.

Much of a meditation practice is simply the commitment to be regularly present with yourself. For this reason, be intentional about when and where you will do this practice on a daily basis. I recommend sitting upright in a chair or on a cushion or pillow, and at a time when you won't be distracted, such as early morning, your lunch break, or before bed. I caution against laying down because you don't want to fall asleep. Position yourself in an intentionally aware and presence-inducing posture, as if to affirm to the universe, "I am right here, right now."

Step 2: Begin with a scope in mind.

Set a timer or use a meditation app. (I prefer the timed meditation on the free version of the Calm app available on the App Store.) When you are first getting started, choose a period of time that feels achievable, one in which you can commit to being with yourself without interruption. That could be three, five, or seven minutes to start. Ideally, you'll want to work up to at least fifteen minutes, but start with whatever time frame works for you.

Because my household consists of two lovely children, two demanding dogs, and an ambitious and restless husband, I have found that the best time and place for me to meditate is immediately upon waking, before the rest of the household wakes. In my bedroom on my meditation cushion at 5:30 a.m., while my husband is sound asleep next to me, I sit for at least twenty minutes of practice daily. This is my commitment to myself. Choosing this time has made it so that meditation is now naturally a part of my morning wake-up routine.

Step 3: Focus and begin.

Pick one point of focus that will be your anchor. Start the timer. And begin your meditation.

Your anchor is the thing you come back to in your practice. A very common anchor is the breath—observing both the "in" and "out" breath from your nose or mouth without thought. Or it could be observing the sound of the fan in the room. It could also be deciding to be present to the throbbing of your heartbeat in your chest. Or it could simply be that you intend to be acutely present to the sound of silence around you.

Your job for your meditation is to be with your anchor without any analyzing or judging thoughts. But the reality is that you won't be able to stay there for long. Before you know it, you'll be thinking. It might sound like this, *Hmm, I wonder if I'm doing this right. Is this what meditation is supposed to feel like? Hmm. I remember Aunt Alice telling me years ago about her meditation retreat in India. Wow. India. Wouldn't it be fun to go there! Oh, and the food. Ooo, now I'm hungry. We should order Indian tonight! Oh shoot, that reminds me, I need to go to the grocery store . . .*

Thought streams are just going to happen, so don't resist it. Your job is to catch that you're thinking. What point you are in the thought stream doesn't matter, as long as you commit to catching it when you can.

Oh! I'm thinking about my grocery list! Back to my breath . . .

And back to your breath you go, or the sound of the fan, or whatever your anchor is. You'll be with your anchor for however long you are (maybe twenty seconds?) before you start thinking again. No bother. Just continue to catch and come back until you hear the ending bell or timer of your meditation.

As you practice these three basic steps, it's important not to overlay any labels or judgment about your process before, during, or after your session. In other words,

- **Before your session:** Drop any and all hopes, expectations, or worries about the session you are entering. Allow yourself to be as spacious as silence itself.

- **During your meditation:** Commit to being with your anchor. Catch when you're thinking and come back to your anchor as much as you can. If you catch yourself thinking only once during a fifteen-minute meditation, great! If you catch yourself and come back seven times, great! If you don't catch it at all, great! The idea is that you are present with yourself, committed to practicing compassionate awareness during a chosen period of time, and that you hold this as a sacred practice with *and for* yourself.

- **After the session:** Let it be what it is. Have no label such as good or bad, right or wrong, wanted or unwanted. Honor your experience as being on purpose, because remember, it's always working out for you!

Let's Get the Story Straight about Meditation

If we can clear up some of the mistaken beliefs about what meditating really is and how it works, we just might be able to change your relationship to it enough that you make it part of your daily routine.

Let's just break this down. The following four roadblocks are all the ways that we talk ourselves out of meditating. They are the myths and misconceptions that you can be free of.

Roadblock #1: "I'm doing it wrong."

Yes, meditating is about quieting the mind. But our minds are really busy, and thoughts happen without us willing them. The goal is to be *with* your mind, not take control of it in meditation. Let your thoughts come and go—*meditating is not attaching to them*. Someone gave me a great analogy once: imagine sitting on an overpass of a freeway and watching the cars zoom by beneath you. Imagine each of those cars is one of your thoughts. Regular inner dialogue is akin to hopping off that overpass onto each approaching car and zooming away with it. Regular life is being lost in thought. Meditating is *noticing* the thoughts, not identifying with them, not being invested in them, and not judging them. It's anchoring yourself on that overpass and watching them pass by.

Meditating is going to feel clunky because our minds are a mess! Unless we put in over 40,000 lifetimes hours of rigorous meditation, * we'll never get to a point where we consistently exist in a blissful abyss for the entire session. Know that each session will be different—some being more peaceful, some being really loud and consuming—and that

---

*Daniel Goleman and Richard J. Davidson, *Altered Traits: Science Reveals How Meditation Changes Your Mind, Brain, and Body* (New York: Penguin Random House, 2017).

continued

is how it goes. Practice being nonresistant to what arises. Our work is to *intend* to be present with whatever emerges and come back to the chosen focus of our meditation practice. Many choose the breath as an anchor to come back to, and some choose choice-less awareness of what is in our experience (sounds, sensations, etc.). Either is fine, and you can't get it wrong. But you *do* need to practice.

Roadblock #2: "There's something to get that I'm not getting."
Instead of thinking about meditation as something to get right, or as a means to an end, think about it as mental, emotional, and spiritual hygiene. Think of it this way: How do you feel about brushing your teeth? Do you hem and haw every time you have to brush your teeth? Do you resent it and complain that it takes up too much time? Do you criticize yourself for not doing it perfectly? Do you report to others when you brush your teeth because it's that noteworthy?

No, you probably have no story around brushing your teeth. You do it because you're committed to the practice of it, you know it's good for you, and though you reap no big rewards each time you do it, you still do it anyway. You know it's serving you in the short and long term. It's nothing to write home about, yet it's something that is important enough to commit to daily.

What if you had *that* relationship to meditating? What if it were such a simple self-care practice that, while perhaps nothing to get excited over, it's something you commit to doing because it's for your own good.

Roadblock #3: "I don't have the time."
Baloney. Seriously. When we say we don't have the time, what we're really saying is, "This isn't a priority given the time I have." You just have to decide that *you* matter enough to channel fifteen or so minutes of your day in this way. Fifteen minutes is nothing in the big scheme

of things. And if you really can't find fifteen minutes in your day (15!), then doesn't that tell you that you need meditation more than ever?

If you are struggling to make this self-care practice a priority given the time you have, I would encourage you to check your screen time stats on your smartphone to prove to yourself that you do actually have fifteen minutes to spare. Once you learn that you're averaging seven hours and twenty-one minutes a day on your phone, you might be compelled to allocate fifteen minutes of that block to your self-care. However, it will require that you make a minor trade-off: fifteen minutes spent in meditation or fifteen minutes scrolling through videos on TikTok? You'll have to decide it's worth it.

When you commit and see this through for even just a few weeks, you'll find that your increased self-awareness and new access to *choice* will compel you to stay the course. You'll quickly discover that the benefits outweigh the time commitment and time no longer becomes the roadblock.

Now, if after this you're *still* struggling to find the time, then time is not the excuse. It's that you think it's too boring.

Roadblock #4: "It's boring."

It's boring only if you think of meditating as a means to an end. (Think teeth-brushing again.) Viewing it through a wider lens, you'll discover that it's an indispensable process in honoring yourself and growing your self-awareness. Meditating allows you to realize that you have thoughts and that you are not your thoughts. It gives you the ability to choose your focus instead of being victim to the focus you happen to be sustaining. It empowers you to *live* life instead of letting life live you—which is exactly what it means to be always on purpose.

If you commit to seeing this as a practice and not a goal, and you cease to judge or label your process, meditation will just be a thing you do, not a thing you dread.

A FINAL WORD ABOUT LIVING ON PURPOSE

It's been said before that life is our canvas and each one of us is the artist who determines what takes shape upon its textured expanse. Have you noticed how great artists are passionate about their creations and care deeply about bringing them to fruition—and then giving them to the world simply as offerings of truth and beauty? Very much like that, living an always-on-purpose life requires that you care deeply about embodying a knowing of your wholeness and completeness. And so the *moment* you feel any effects of inner opposition, that's your cue to catch it and come back. If you are sensitive to how you feel most often throughout the day, then that's all you need to catch and come back. And your meditation practice will strengthen the self-awareness muscle that will help you to eventually do this with ease.

Like the artist with her favorite tools and her principles for living a creative life, be impassioned about the gifts you have and the choices you get to make. Hold sacred your self-awareness, let your feeling be your guide, refuse to measure yourself or your life against any external standard (according to how you "should" be), and trust that it's always working out for you (even when it doesn't feel like it).

Commit to knowing that you are already complete, not believing it. And claim the life you were born to live.

Which one is that again?

It's the fun one where you get to laugh in the midst of storms. The one where no one loses because you're winning, and when they're winning you still feel like you're winning. The one where clarity, joy, fulfillment, and abundance are your regular experience. It's the one where . . .

Appreciation is your fuel

Joy is your guide

and

Love is your purpose.

A Word Before You Go:

COMMON SIDE EFFECTS OF
THE ON-PURPOSE LIFE

Your life lived on purpose is the best kind because it's your unique expression of consciousness, rooted in truth and shared generously with the world around you. And making the subtle yet epic choice to know that not one thing is missing—that you are everything you ever hoped to be and more—comes with some lovely consequences that you should be aware of as you prepare to close this book.

UNCONDITIONAL COMPASSION

When you come to *know* your unconditional wholeness, you can't help but know it in everyone. You look around at all those you encounter on a day-to-day basis and you feel a compassion, a curiosity, and a deep familiarity, recognizing that you're bonded beyond appearances, stories, fears, and survival mechanisms. You see that we are all connected in our origins of unconditional wholeness and that the entirety of our humanity is trying to come back to that miraculous source point.

All of us turn from truth. All of us find ways to survive the pain we experience as human beings. All of us find ways to survive the painful false beliefs that *compound* our pain. All of us learn to ride the roller coaster of conditions. And all of us want to feel good. And perhaps more importantly, all of us want to rest in the knowing that we belong. You're acutely aware of this now. And when you look around and observe everyone in all contexts: postal workers, leaders, grocery clerks, scientists, librarians, celebrities, landscapers, politicians, teachers, fellow shoppers, fellow parents, and all the people you've never met, you feel an unconditional compassion and appreciation for our shared journey.

UNCONDITIONAL CONNECTION

This compassion opens the door to a strange yet amazing feeling—everyone feels like a friend you just don't know yet. Even if you've never seen them before in your life. Even if they aren't overwhelmingly friendly. Why? Because you *know* their wholeness and completeness to the core. And you don't need to know the details of their life to know this because it is the *unconditional* truth. With this comes the understanding that their acts and their behaviors have nothing to do with you. Other people's behaviors cease to be triggering. In the place of objective and compassionate observation, you don't take their actions personally, you see that their behavior is the result of the relationship they have with themselves. With any and all that you encounter, you welcome a budding connection that is bound to flourish given you put in the time and effort. With this sense of authentic connection, compassionate discernment arises too. You'll lovingly discern who to invest in and who not to. No judgment about it, just clarity. Regardless of your preference for their company or not, each person you encounter is honored for the magical mystery they are—already and always worthy of connection, love, and belonging.

FEARLESSNESS

Our biology is built to keep us safe from environmental and social threats, and our brain will signal danger even if danger isn't present. That results in the feeling of fear. While we can't eliminate those biological signals (and we wouldn't want to!), we do experience a significant reduction in our fear of failure and rejection. Remember, when you *know* your wholeness, then you're not seeing through inner opposition lenses. With clear eyes, the stuff of life doesn't mean anything! When mistakes mean nothing about you, you're not afraid of them, because it's not proof about *you*. In other words, when you know your wholeness, and you *get* that every single person on the planet is hardwired to feel a sense of belonging, then you can't help but put yourself out there and take bigger risks for the sake of making the world a better place. You're abundant, joyous, and prosperous in all your endeavors because you genuinely understand that nothing can be taken from you. From a place of truth, you only have love to give, and you're unafraid to give it.

APPRECIATION

When you know there is no way things *should* be, you are left with *what is*. You drop into a state of presence with whatever is in front of you. And appreciation for what is can be felt in a profound way. As you dance with life with little resistance and no inner opposition, all that is left in the place of drama is awe, wonder, and gratitude for our moment-to-moment experience.

ENTHUSIASM

That feeling of appreciation doesn't stop at contentment. It leads to action. From a place of gratitude, your desire to have more impact and be of more service to others becomes a predominant stance. When your focus is no longer on you, your life feels purposeful and meaningful, and a natural excitement for *what could be* emerges. You get that you are in a continual process of unfolding and your enthusiasm for creating more life, love, and experiences drives you forward.

JOY BEYOND WORDS

Living on purpose, from your whole and complete self—unconditionally—is a grand feeling no words can accurately capture. With more time and energy, life is just easier. You now live a life of mellow magic. You are already the person you've been looking for and striving to be, and so now you can just have fun with it all! It's your priority now to be easy with yourself, to find reasons to laugh, and to decide daily that you're worth every moment of life's thrilling journey.

All these states of being are the natural outgrowth of you blossoming into the fullness of yourself. And how could it be otherwise? You are a precious, worthy, and deserving soul here to do great things. My whole and complete being sees the whole and complete being in you, unconditionally. I'm delighted we're in this together—always, and on purpose.

ACKNOWLEDGMENTS

My life lived on purpose is possible because of the people who have shaped me, supported me, and loved me—most importantly my family.

A deepest thank you to my husband, Arnold. Your unconditional love, support, and belief in me has made all this possible. You make everything possible. You make everything better. You make me better.

To my incredible kids, Aidan and Aila, you have gifted me with perspective that infuses my purpose with love and life. Thank you for being the beautiful and delightful souls that you are. I am lucky to be your mama and I love you more than words could ever express.

To my parents, Abby and Russ, thank you for loving, guiding, and supporting me to become the woman I am today. You're the best mom and dad anyone could ever ask for. You continually inspire me to greatness.

And to my brother and sister, your support means the world. Jake, thanks for always believing in me and being such a bright, positive light. Kate, thanks for your huge heart—your real and *honest* heart. You are the reason I am *not* crossing my arms and leaning against a counter.

To all my clients who let me into your lives to be a part of your transformation, your partnership has been an honor and a privilege. I have grown tremendously as a result of our conversations. And to those clients and dear friends who consistently requested that I put our conversations in book form, I thank you from the bottom of my heart. Your loving insistence not only planted the seed but nourished this book into existence.

KC Harris got the ball rolling and encouraged movement in the direction of becoming an "author" when he approached me after one of my keynotes. Thank you for becoming the best and most fun sidekick ever, transforming the idea to an inevitability.

Shauna Shapiro, thank you for being a powerful catalyst for magic. Kristine Carlson, who became my book doula and soul sister, continually guides me with enthusiasm, love, wisdom, and joy. You are my goddess-mama-sister-friend. Life is so much better with you in it.

Debra Evans, my angelic and brilliant editor, melded with my heart and vision fully. Deb poured through every chapter I wrote, enhancing my words with her heartful literary magic, and partnered with me with love, eagerness, encouragement, and humor. Thank you, Deb, for your loving and collaborative spirit. You singlehandedly made the challenges of writing a book one of the most nourishing and joyful experiences of my life, which obviously include forever sisterhood and dolphin sightings.

Bethany Saltman's keen eye, friendship, and encouragement kept me hopeful (and honest!) throughout the writing process. Thank you, friend, for keeping me sane as a writer *and* a mama.

It's quite a feat to bring a book to life, and I have a large team to thank for that. Thank you, Emily Mills, for your illustrations, and Shawn Habermehl, for your photography. I can't wait to partner with you both on the next project. To the good people of Greenleaf Book Group, you have been true partners through and through. Deepest gratitude to David Endris, Lindsay Bohls, Lindsey Clark, Anne Sanow, Diana Coe, Sheila Parr, Corrin Foster, Evelyn Sher, Amanda Marquette, and Kristine Peyre-Ferry. Your expertise, support, and encouragement have been incredibly appreciated. I couldn't have done this without you all.

And to all my treasured friends and family who, in your generous and unique ways, played a powerful part in the manifestation of my path and/or this book, thank you. Whether it was your encouragement, support, ideas, opinions, mentoring, coaching, or loving guidance along the way, it meant a lot and you've made a big difference. In no particular order: Mike Robbins, Peter Coughlan, Marta Maria Marraccini, Soken Graf, Marc Nicolson, Maurizio and Zaya Benazzo, Adrienne Whitmore, Sarah Marshall, Lisa and Chris Farmer, Cheri Scalzi, Rahnie Smith, Ashley Rosales, Andrea Rosario, Gail Allen, Monali Joshi, Erin Weitzenberg, Suzy Lee, Heather and Tom Lofthouse, Morley Boyer, Meghan Gendelman, Britta Williams, Carla Detchon, Maxim Williams, Chrissy Roth-Francis, Kim Nicol, Dan Moriarty, Robin Kahn, Tim Fortesque, Bryan Lemos, Dashaun Simmons, Kristina Barnes, Christine Sarkis, Betsy Flanagan, Sheila Buchanan, Jordan Howard, Karen Loenser, Mandip Kudhail, Epiphany and Austin Shaw, Jerzy and Aniela Gregorek, Heather Hood, Vien Truong, Jazzie Newton, Karen Salmansohn, and Jenn and Marcus DePaula.

Lastly—within, before, and among it all is the presence of great teachers. Special thanks to these individuals whose work has profoundly influenced my thinking: Wayne Dyer; Esther and Abraham Hicks; Thich Naht Hahn; Ervin Laszlo, PhD; Stephen Porges, PhD, Robert Lanza, MD; Daniel Siegel, MD; David Bohm, PhD; Bruce Lipton, PhD; Fred Alan-Wolf, PhD; Gabor Mate, MD; and Judith E. Glaser. Thank you for providing the inspiration that guides me. In the way that your work has touched me deeply, I aspire to do the same for others.

ABOUT THE AUTHOR

*A*my Eliza Wong is the founder of Always On Purpose®. She is a transformational coach and facilitator working with the biggest names in tech, organizations such as Salesforce, Facebook, LinkedIn, and more. Amy offers transformative leadership development and cutting-edge communication strategies not only to executives and corporate teams around the world, but also in the halls of academia, with institutions such as Stanford University and the University of California at Berkeley. Amy pulls from various disciplines, studies, and practices to find an integrative approach to achieving genuine and lasting success—what she refers to as "the fundamentals of thriving."

As a keynote speaker, Amy is in demand for her authenticity, charisma, depth, and an incisive approach to addressing topics that matter. She moves and inspires both individuals and groups to take the risk to change and come to know their fullest potential. Amy has an intense passion for helping people experience meaningful joy and satisfaction in their daily lives, free of fear and false perception. In short, she thrives on helping others live and lead *on purpose*.

For more than twenty years, Amy has devoted herself to the study and practice of transformation. As a certified Executive Coach using expertise in transpersonal psychology, design thinking, interpersonal neurobiology, and Conversational Intelligence®, Amy has provided thousands of transformative experiences for individuals, executives, teams, and organizations.

Amy graduated from UC Berkeley with a BA in mathematics and has an MA in transpersonal psychology from Sofia University. When she's not coaching, writing, and speaking, Amy spends time in Berkeley, California, with her husband, two children, and two dogs.